Three Days in Damascus

A Memoir by Kim Schultz

Palewell Press

Three Days in Damascus – a Memoir

Printed and bound in the United Kingdom

Published by Palewell Press http://palewellpress.co.uk

First Edition

ISBN 978-0-9955351-0-7

All Rights Reserved. Copyright ©2016 Kim Schultz. No part of this publication may be reproduced or transmitted in any form or by any means, without permission in writing from the author.

Front cover painting Copyright © Omar Odeh 2016

Front cover photo of painting www.crimsoncatstudios.com

Front cover photograph Copyright © Kim Schultz 2016

Cover design Copyright © Sheridan Reeve 2016

Palewell Press supports the Forest Stewardship Council® (FSC®) the leading international forest-certification organisation. Our books carrying the FSC® label are printed on FSC®-certified paper. Their printing and binding complies with ISO 14001 (Environmental Management) and 50001 (Energy Management)

"You cannot save people. You can only love them."
Anais Nin

This book is dedicated to Omar and all the
Iraqis who let me share their story

Introduction

In 2009, my friend Kim Schultz and I both experienced life-altering events. That was the year Kim went to the Middle East on a fact-finding mission with the NGO, Intersections International. As part of a multi-disciplinary group of artists, Kim traveled to Syria, Lebanon and Jordan to meet with Iraqi refugees living throughout the region. She spent a month listening to stories by family after family who had been driven from their homes by actual or threatened violence. Old people, young people, married with children, or childless. People who had, at one time, led relatively normal lives, cumulative impact of 13 years of U.S.-led sanctions on their country's infrastructure notwithstanding. By the time Kim had arrived on the scene, the collapse of their government after the removal of Saddam Hussein (also by U.S. troops), had led to Iraq's total descent into tribal warfare.

And it was during her time in Syria that Kim met Omar, an Iraqi artist, also a refugee. And over the course of three days, they fell in love.

Between the visceral impact of confronting the human toll of decades of U.S. policy on Iraqi civilians and, well, falling in love with an Iraqi refugee who was trapped in limbo, Kim arrived back in New York City pretty shattered. And while she was busy having her world turned upside down, I'd gone through my own kind of looking glass. While Kim was out of the country, my husband had died, in a rapid decline after a lifelong battle with a chronic illness.

It was weeks before she and I spoke, both of us too numb to go beyond emailing the words, "We have to talk."

Back in 1999-2001, I had worked on developing a documentary film called "Christmas in Baghdad." I'd been exploring the impact of economic sanctions on the civilian population of Iraq as well as their family members now living in the United States, in the years before Saddam Hussein had been taken out of power. I'd been tracking the activities of anti-sanctions activists across the United States, people engaging in non-violent protests against these U.S.-led policies that were hurting so many innocent people.

A combination of events in 2001, including several deaths in my family and the geopolitical earthquake of 9/11, effectively derailed production of that film. But my sense of solidarity with the Iraqi ex-pats and refugees I had met and interviewed during shooting was still very much alive.

A shell-shocked Kim was now faced with the task of creating a theatrical performance out of her Middle East odyssey. She had taken on the same challenge as I had a decade earlier - to share the stories of Iraqi people with an American audience in a way that served to underscore our common humanity. Sadly, the drumbeat of war six years earlier had conflated Iraq and its people with the perpetrators of 9/11. Fueled by a deliberate misinformation campaign carried out by members of our government and most major media outlets, a large swath of Americans actually believed that Iraq was somehow behind the events of that awful day. In truth, there was no such connection until we took out Saddam Hussein. That's when the enemies of the west developed a stronghold in what became a chaotic and leaderless country. There was no Al-Qaeda in Iraq prior to the downfall of Saddam Hussein's Ba'ath Party.

Baghdad, in its heyday, was a cosmopolitan city, an international destination. Iraq had been a primarily secular nation, not a fundamentalist Muslim country. Women were relatively liberated, enjoying higher education and the same variety of occupations as men. Most young people attended college. The medical system was as sophisticated and high tech as any in Europe or North America. People lived relatively comfortable lives, motivated by familiar ideals such as providing a good education and comfortable home for their children, enjoying music and art and other forms of cultural expression. Iraqis are some of the more thoughtful and intellectual people I've met - gracious, generous and rooted in a deep cultural tradition that dates back to the beginnings of modern civilization.

But all of that changed. Long standing rivalries between different ethnic groups - Sunni, Shia and the Kurds of the north - kept under wraps during Saddam Hussein's repressive regime, were now free to flourish. Armed militias sprang up everywhere. Women, frequent targets of harassment, resorted to wearing the hijab under threat of violence from religious extremists. Neighbors turned against neighbors as violence permeated everyday life. Kidnappings and murders became commonplace, and people no longer knew who to trust. Whatever semblance of civility had existed before slowly disintegrated, to be replaced by the savagery of thugs on all sides. Individuals who had worked as translators and drivers for the US military were especially targeted - branded as traitors. The wheels were coming off the bus.

Kim was now facing the same uphill battle that I had faced - the deceptively difficult task of convincing Americans that Iraqis are people, too. But Kim had something that I did not. Something that would prove a powerful tool in hooking people into an emotional journey that would open their hearts and minds. Kim had a love story.

"No Place Called Home," the one-woman show that Kim wrote and performed as a result of her Middle East sojourn, is a collection of heartbreaking stories culled from her myriad interviews with Iraqi refugees, wrapped in the love story of her relationship with Omar. That play formed the basis for the book you are about to read.

I won't tell you how this love story ends - we rarely know how anything ends. What I do know is that some things that end can never be recovered. My husband is gone. The Iraq of days gone by is dead. These deaths are permanent. The question is, how do we recover from losses that seem so incalculable?

These days the world is also grappling with the fate of Syrian refugees, who have taken so much of the global spotlight. But the facts about Iraqi refugees are as overwhelming as their Syrian counterparts. 5,000,000 Iraqis now live displaced from their homes. The country they once knew and loved is largely destroyed. The death and destruction that has taken place was the result of economic policies followed by military actions that overwhelmingly impacted the civilians of that nation. We are left to wonder how this happened on our watch, and what we can do to restore some semblance of balance to this ravaged part of the world - in the same way that Kim has been left to wonder how to restore balance to her life after it was ravaged by an unparalleled love and passion, not only for Omar, but for all the Iraqis she met.

Perhaps it's easier for us to wrap our brains around a story that centers on only two people instead of millions. Maybe as we examine the twists and turns in Kim and Omar's love story, we'll find clues as to how to manage unprecedented, seismic shifts in our own lives. My wish for Kim, and Omar, and the rest of the Iraqi people, is that the kind of insights we can glean from their story are the kind that open the possibility for a promising future for them all.

Deborah Oster Pannell
October, 2016

Contents

This true story takes place in Lebanon, Jordan, Syria, New York, Mexico and Canada over a period of 3 years, starting in 2009.

Map of travels in the story

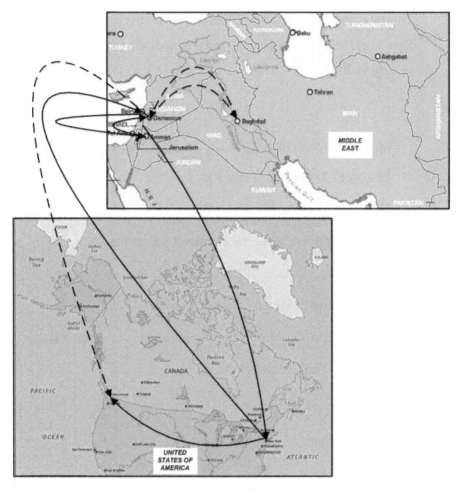

Kim's journey is the solid line starting in New York.

Omar's journey is the dotted line starting in Damascus and ending in Vancouver.

Prologue - Three Hour Plane Ride

I refuse to let my story end with an arranged marriage. That's ridiculous—I'm from Minnesota. We don't do arranged marriages.

* * *

So here I am sitting in the window seat of an Air Canada flight looking out at the fast-approaching city of Vancouver. The clouds disappear as we pass through them, and white, snowy earth starts to appear. I look down at the grid-like pattern beginning to show itself. Omar is down there somewhere and after three years, I am finally going to see him. Holy. Crap. (Or whatever the Arabic equivalent is.)

I try to breathe. 30,000 feet up in the air, flying toward my past or toward my future, I try to breathe. Will this be the beginning or the end with Omar? Ironically, it is New Year's—an auspicious time of both beginnings and ends, and I need one or the other. I have no more room in my life for middle. I've had three *years* of middle. Three years of

3

international phone calls, emails and IMs. Three years of an on-again/off-again pseudo-relationship. Three years of "he is too far," "we are too different," "this is too hard." Three years of questions. I am sick to *death* of questions and I am sick to death of middle. I need it to begin—or end. Honestly, either way is fine with me. *I just need an answer.* Part of me suspects and even *expects* the end. I mean, let's be real. But I refuse to end it like it is—in an arranged marriage that doesn't in any way involve me. I want a different ending. And I am going to Vancouver to find it.

I focus once again on the approaching city. It is getting closer. Inhale. Exhale. My stomach begins to somersault—massive, Olympic-style somersaults.

O. Lympic. O. Mar. O. My God.

I've waited a long time for this reunion. I fought for it through war, revolution and yes…an arranged marriage for this chance at love—unforeseen, unlikely, unimaginable love.

The pilot flips on the 'fasten seat belt' light and we begin our final approach. How did I end up falling so hard for this Iraqi?

Three Weeks in the Middle East

This story has never been easy.

I wish it was. I mean, the love story part is easy. But I really can't tell you the love story without telling you everything—from the beginning to the end. Otherwise you won't understand. You won't understand why I tried so hard, for so long. Why it happened at all.

This is, after all, a story of beginnings and endings. A story of three days, three weeks, three months, three hours, three years. A story waiting to end...or maybe waiting to begin. A story that isn't supposed to be a love story.

So maybe I have to start at the beginning. No, wait— the coffee grounds! That's where I should start—the stupid, life-changing coffee grounds.

Let's go back.

It was the end of a month long trip to the Middle East to interview Iraqi refugees, and after three weeks of listening to the stories no one should ever have to hear, let alone live, I was drowning in helplessness and heartache.

Late one afternoon, after another long and tiring day in Damascus, in another broken down, overly-populated home of Iraqi refugees, after telling us another frustratingly preventable story, a little old Iraqi grandmother offered to read my coffee grounds.

What?

Yes. Absolutely yes.

I love stuff like that: tea leaves, Tarot cards, palm readings, horoscopes, Magic 8 balls—you name it, I love it. I'd prefer you to tell me my future rather than for me to figure it out. Easier that way.

And so, once I heard about this magical mystic, I immediately slammed the last of my coffee, careful to not swallow any of the requisite grounds. Thank God they offered coffee, not tea this time. The stars were aligned. There was no way I was gonna miss the opportunity – a reading from a future-seeing, fortune-telling Babylonian … old person?

The grandmother gestured to me to flip my cup onto the saucer. I did as I was told, of course. I looked up at her expectantly as she took my cup, giddy with excitement. Yes. Tell me my future, woman! I'm ready!

She swirled the remaining grounds and studied the design. I waited. My God, what could it be? She looked at me and tipped the cup again. I waited some more. Finally, she spoke: Arabic. Damn it! Always Arabic! (You'd think we were in the Middle East or something.) I raised my eyebrows eagerly at the translator. She hurriedly translated.

"There is someone in your family sick. A male…"

Oh my Lord, my sweet grandfather was just admitted to the hospital for pneumonia. I just found out yesterday. Yes! Yes! She's good. I tell ya, she's good.

The translator continued for my seer. "You will come into money."

Well, good heavens. Who doesn't like to hear that? Excellent. Keep it comin' lady.

And then the grandmother looked deep into the grounds: swirl, swirl, swirl. She tipped the cup, found a new angle and at last, smiled, looked me straight in the eye and spoke with all her ancient wisdom…in Arabic, of course.

The Arabic-speaking room reacted in small smiles and shared glances, but my translator for some reason went silent.

What did she say? What did she say? For God's sake, translator, translate! That's your one job on this Earth. Translate!

The translator smiled at me and after a pause finally said, "You will meet a man soon, whom you will marry." I looked at her, eyebrows raised. She continued, "You will be engaged to this man, perhaps after a very short time."

"When will I meet him?" I asked.

"Soon, very soon. Maybe even in Damascus soon."

Really?

Sah-weet.

Later that night, I met Omar.

Damn coffee grounds.

*   *   *

My colleagues and I were at an event set up by our hosting non-profit. It was an early evening meet-and-greet of sorts between American artists and Iraqi refugee artists, an opportunity to talk and share as artists, without any other labels. Thankfully it was also a happy hour, and I for one was happy…for the alcohol. In this region, there is limited access to a much-needed-glass-of-wine at the end of a traumatic and trying day. (Although every day, it seemed, was traumatic and trying.) But today especially was. Just a few more days in Damascus and I was headed back to New York—to process, write and get back to my normal life B.R. (Before-Refugees).

As if that would be possible. As if that would ever be possible.

In the meantime, there we were—Americans and Iraqis—in a very old, underground art gallery awkwardly looking at each other, all of us secretly hoping not to have to respectively hear or tell another sad, sad story; all of us just waiting for the alcohol part to start, when I saw Omar. And damn it all—if he didn't see me back.

He was so...Iraqi.

Dark-skinned, dark-eyed and...Iraqi. Oh, Middle Eastern men! I did not know you were my weakness! But clearly you are. Or at least *he* is. I looked across the room into Omar's ridiculously beautiful, piercing and yes, Iraqi eyes and he looked back. I mean he *really* looked back. Crap.

Crap. Crap. Crap. Crap. Crap. Crap. Crap.

The connection was immediate, intense and impossible. Absolutely impossible. And possibly unethical...

Oh. My...

Omar.

Somehow Omar and I made it through the cumbersome and unnecessarily long group introductions, all the while sneaking furtive and flirty glances. Was he the man in the grounds? Was he my coffee ground man? At last the bar opened and the mingling part began. Thank. God.

Then as if sharing a dance, or maybe just a well-used cliché, we slowly meandered to the mahogany bar circling each other and the room, moving in and out as if partners on a dance floor. The tension was palpable as we finally closed in. I forced myself to remember to breathe. Just breathe. Time slowed to a halt, until at last we were standing directly across from each other. It was like magnets, like pita to hummus, like…inevitability.

Omar smiled and time returned to normal. Damn. That smile. *I was thirty-nine years old and had never felt that before. Nothing like that. Ever.* Damn.

We stared at each other a while longer—Omar and I— maybe ten seconds, maybe a century—hard to tell. Eyes locked, we were so torturously, inappropriately close, that I could feel his breath. I paused, my heart pounding—pert near out of my chest. I hoped he didn't notice. Maybe he would just think it was the beat of the Middle Eastern oud music playing in the background. I thought, what is this song? Whatever it is, it is now our song. (Note to self: find out song) I wondered if I was allowed to fall for a refugee I was here to officially meet. Too late.

"Omar, I'm Kim," I finally blurted out, unable to hold it together anymore.

"I know," he said, and smiled. Is he magic? How does he know? Oh right. Group introductions. Doy.

Other artists joined us and we managed some stilted small talk, until Omar asked, "Would you like see my paintings sometime, Kim?"

"Yes, very much," I smiled and noticing the others, guiltily added, "I would like to see all of your paintings. I wish I could!" The others in the circle smiled vaguely, not yet fluent in bullshit.

He said something in Arabic to his friends. They looked at me smiling broadly. "What did you say?" I gently accused.

"I said I wondered if you were married, or...?" Omar admitted quite daringly. I awkwardly looked at the artist to my left and then to my right. They both smiled at me. My heart pounding got louder. Good lord, did he just ask me that in front of everyone? What is happening right now?

As if reading my mind, he responded, "Don't worry. No one else really speak English here."

"Oh," I sighed with relief, and then, "But wait, you said it in Arabic."

He just smiled. Bastard.

And then with my own coy smile, I responded, "I'm single."

We shared something highly resembling a moment. I desperately looked somewhere else to break it, anywhere else. I watched the oud player for a while. I looked at the bar. I looked at the floor. Omar and the other artists exchanged some words in Arabic and I drank my wine, trying to calm my heart and assess the situation.

This is nothing. I'm exaggerating. Calm down. This is nothing, Kim. Harmless flirting.

"Kim," I heard Omar call to me, jarring me out of my thoughts. He was holding a small piece of paper.

As he passed me his card with contact information, coffee grounds in motion, our fingers brushed against each other, touching for the first time. This is *not* nothing. This is *something*. He smiled at me again—a smile to launch a thousand ships, a thousand war ships.

He is from Iraq, after all.

*   *   *

"I have lost my husband, it seems," said Sarah, smiling—incessantly, inappropriately smiling. "He went back to Iraq over year ago and I have not heard from him."

Sarah was the last interview in a difficult day of interviews, and through no fault of her own, she was trying my nerves. It was the day after the night I met Omar, and we had a small pre-arranged "date" back at the hotel that afternoon to go to his studio and see his paintings. I had a date with Omar. Holy crapoly. So my head was swirling, my heart was thumping and dammit, this Sarah seemed just fine. At this point in the trip, I had met a lot of refugees, and she seemed a-ok. I mean, don't get me wrong she was still a shattered refugee, but…

…my mind was crazy distracted with thoughts of Omar and his amazing brown, almond-shaped eyes—even in the midst of all the devastation.

In my defense, it had been a long month and I was desperate for distraction, drowning in this world of refuge, and Omar seemed to be the perfect life preserver. So gratefully, I swam in thoughts of Omar, away from *all* the refugees toward just my one.

I tried to focus. We were in a seemingly upscale, middle class apartment. I mean, it was pretty nice—one of the best I'd seen. Sarah's children were in the kitchen making us the requisite tea as I sat on a fancy sofa, next to the actually decorated walls. The place had pictures. Hell, the place had walls—a step up from some of the refugee homes out there.

I kept thinking about the family of nine living in a square one-room cinder block house that we'd met earlier today. They had nothing, literally nothing, except for a half bag of rice in the corner. I couldn't get that cinder block family off my mind.

Okay, I admit, I was judging Sarah for seemingly having so much compared to the cinder block family or most of the other Iraqis I met. But honestly, it was just the last interview of the day, and I was desperate to blow that Popsicle stand (or whatever the Arabic equivalent is) and go find Omar.

And this *Sarah*...wouldn't stop smiling. It reminded me of Omar's smile. Damn. Omaaaaar. I was so excited to see him later that I couldn't focus. Sarah caught my eye and smiled again. Why is she smiling so much, I thought to myself, and what is she saying, anyway? I really should listen.

"He was hit by car bomb and half his face was paralyzed. We had to leave Iraq to get medical treatment, as there are no more doctors in Iraq. But before he could get this treatment, his mother fell ill and he had to return to Iraq." She paused here, but then continued unfazed. "It has been one year since I hear from him. I try everything to find him, of course. He is my husband, after all! Police, hospital, his mother! No one knows anything. Nothing. Maybe U.S. Army has taken my husband to keep him safe. Maybe, yes? Insha'Allah..."

Insha'Allah: God willing or with God's help—one of the newly acquired words I added to my growing Arabic dictionary.

I paused, taking in what she said.

She must know how unlikely this is, but it's her lifeline, her life preserver in her constant fear of going under. Yes, we all nodded, keeping her afloat. "Insha'Allah." Now I was listening.

"I tell lie to my children," Sarah softly confessed, checking the hall for her children. "I pretend to be on the phone with their father sometimes. I have imaginary conversations with nobody on the other side, so my children, they not worry and so they will behave. My children behave better it seems, if they think their father will be mad. So I lie. I pretend to talk to their father, pretend he is alive. I am afraid to tell them the truth…"

At last, the smile faded.

"…to tell them to no longer wait, that he is not…coming home."

So she knew.

I could no longer breathe. The waters were perfectly still as we all took in that last little bit. I looked at Sarah, seeing her for the first time. She deserved that. She was fairly young, quite beautiful, with dark flowing hair and big, brown eyes filling now with tears. I watched, but none dropped. For a year, she has pretended to talk to a dead husband on the phone to save them all from having to confront the truth. I was blindsided. I didn't see that coming and it hit me like the current. I gasped under the approaching wave for air. And still, her tear did not drop.

And then mere moments after this brutal admission, this dead stop, her feet back under her—she was fine, smiling again, tear tucked away. She was back in control. I however, was not.

The children returned and served our tea in silence, none of us able to say anything. After some minutes, I excused myself to the small balcony through a sliding glass door, claiming to need fresh air.

This has been a *trip* and not being able to hold it in anymore, I started to cry, sob in fact. But because I didn't want anyone behind me in the room to see I was crying, I tried earnestly to only sob on the front side of my body. I front-side sobbed on a balcony in Damascus, desperate to hide the emotion, to tuck my tears away. I caught my breath and looked to the sky for a sense of familiarity, for peace, for something. But nothing.

I felt guilty. It wasn't my life. It wasn't my story. I shouldn't have been crying, front-side or otherwise. I shouldn't have been *losing* it in front of a woman who *refused* to lose it. But I couldn't help it. I couldn't stop. So I continued to cry until it finally passed. It certainly wasn't the first time I cried on the trip and wouldn't be the last. But my God, how much can one person take?

The cinder block family raced though my head, as did Saleema and Daoud, Raheel, Hatm, the blue shirt man and Najah and her already dead children. And of course Fakher, always Fakher. They were all around me—dancing, sobbing, waiting.

I took in a big breath of the heavy Syrian summer air. It was too much. It was all too much. The wet, hot, humid air…and this. All of it.

The Iraqis deserve more. They deserve better. They deserve *something.*

I was drowning. I don't want to do this anymore, I thought to myself. I want to go home.

No. It's not that easy. Too many lives are at stake. We have to go further back...back to the beginning, back to where it all started.

We have to start over.

```
========================================
KIM'S ARABIC DICTIONARY first installment:
Yanni/ So or um, a filler word
Ma'asalaama/ Goodbye
Shukran/ Word I say the most here…means thank you
========================================
```

I'm sitting inside my first refugee apartment, well…room. It's basically just a room, waiting for my first real interview. I seem to do a lot of waiting here—just like the refugees, I suppose. But I am hopeful. Also just like the refugees.

We are in Beirut, Lebanon—a beautiful, scenic, war-torn city by the sea. This is our first city and only our second day, but already I feel like I've been here a year. Yesterday we were at a women's shelter on a mountaintop with about 300 Iraqi refugee kids, playing games, doing a few interviews, generally hanging out. We rode up said mountain in a rickety old school bus with them. It was everything you'd imagine that trip to be…in Arabic.

Today is quieter. Thank God. Or Allah. (I mean, when in Rome…)

After a morning in community centers, this is the first real in-home interview, and I'm leading it. I'm a newbie and I'm nervous. I don't want to screw up.

I look around the sparsely decorated room. I still can't believe I'm here. This is crazy. I'm not a journalist or a social worker or anybody else who knows about such things. I'm an artist! I was invited along on this trip as part of an artist delegation with a New York based non-profit organization. Eight of us artists are here to interview Iraqi refugees in three countries: Lebanon, Jordan and Syria. We are supposed to hear their stories and bring them back to American audiences through our respective art forms. I'm the writer. I'm supposed to write a play about this issue.

And I will write a play—about what I don't know. Refugees, I guess. But I know nothing about Iraqis and basically nothing about the Iraq war. I mean, I had to *Google* Iraqi refugees before I came. That's how little I knew.

Remember this was 2009, before ISIS, before the Syrian civil war, before the enormous refugee crisis the world faces today exploded. This was before all that. But it was after we as a nation lost interest in anything having to do with Iraq.

And so, like a shockingly large number of Americans, Iraq had little effect on me. The American war machine and my own liberal, middle class-ness had been very successful in keeping me from feeling any real suffering during this war. So I feel *way* out of my element. I mean, this is only day two and look at me! I am already overwhelmed. What will happen to me in *Syria*, the final leg of this journey? How will I feel then? Will I even make it that long or will I have a nervous breakdown first? Honestly. I am scared of this journey, of where it will take me. I just listen to people tell their stories, over and over. That's it. I feel devastated and guilty and scared for them. How will this ever change for them? I worry it won't.

I take a drag of the dry, dense air. It's hot in here. And the air is so stagnant. I wonder how people can just sit in their homes all day when it's this hot? I'm 'sweatin' to the oldies' here. I wipe my brow and look around, trying to get comfortable. This is the home of an older Iraqi couple. We haven't met them yet. A neighbor told us to just come in, that they would be back soon. And so that's what we did—made ourselves right at home.

It's hot. Have I mentioned that? Sweat-dripping-down-the-back-of-my-knees-hot. That's how hot it is. I sigh, as another drop of sweat beelines down the back of my calf. There are worse things, I know. #firstworldproblems

The apartment is small, with some basic furniture; I've seen better, I've seen worse. Lamps, pictures of their family and of course, a television. Most everyone here has a television! "Surely where we are going won't be *that* different! Surely we'll want our T.V.," they must think before leaving their homes headlong into this unknown exodus.

It's dark in here. Too dark. With the sun setting, it's getting hard to see. I stand and go to flip a switch but nothing happens. Hmm. I sit back down and wipe the sweat from my earlobe. Good Lord. Earlobe sweat.

At last we hear someone coming in the back door. Saleema, maybe sixty-five or seventy years old, enters the living room holding onto her husband, helping him to sit in their plastic patio chairs. These chairs are very typical to this region's refugees. Everyone has plastic patio chairs for indoor furniture. Saleema's happen to be green. She sits herself on the green plastic chair, and then looks at us, a bit winded.

"Ok, yanni, sorry to keep you waiting. I am Saleema and my husband Dauod," she starts, with a tired smile, speaking through the translator. She is very sweet. I immediately like her. I look to her husband. He simply nods, avoiding most eye contact, instead looking down at his hands in his lap.

"I sorry so dark in here. We cannot…yanni, we have no electric." No electricity. I catch myself looking at the T.V. Useless. Now just a dust collector, leftover from better days. Shoulda guessed.

"It very difficult. We live in small room, you see. And my husband is diabeetic. He does not see well. Very difficult." I hear some of the neighborhood children playing outside her door. They all seem very curious about the group of American visitors to their neighborhood.

"I am sorry to not offer you tea. We have no electric. I go to neighbors to get tea, but they…" She shakes her head. "I am sorry."

They went to borrow tea for us? That's why they were late? Man, these Iraqis kill me with their hospitality; a warmer welcome I have never received.

Some children now bravely peek in the window. I smile at them. They shriek and run. Yes, I am scary. Run, children, run.

"We wish to have a better future," she continues. "We would be resettled anywhere. Maybe near my sister in Canada? It would be nice be near her again. Oh! I sorry." She says as she catches me wiping more sweat. "Maybe you are too warm?"

God yes, I've been too warm since landing at the Beirut airport. There hasn't been a moment since arriving that I haven't been 'too warm'. See, I am a little chubby (I hate that word. Big-boned? No, that's worse.) and my "few extra pounds" (better…) are unaccustomed to desert heat. But what does it matter at this point? I'm always hot here and always sweating. The end.

She awaits my response. I shake my head no and smile, pretending to scratch an itch as I surreptitiously wipe the sweat. Dauod clears his throat and I glance over at him. He is wringing his hands. This gesture and the man making it immediately captivate me.

The sun continues to set and Saleema continues to speak. "Our story...is deefficult. Since leaving Iraq and my daughter, I have very little memory, only sadness. Our daughter, our beautiful daughter is still in Kirkuk. I miss her, but she cannot leave. She has two children, our grandchildren. We miss them so. We want to see them again so badly! But they cannot leave and we cannot go back. You see, in Baghdad, Dauod sell alcohol. Now during Saddam, this was fine, but after, after…" Saleema shakes her head here and pauses, a long heavy pause. "Because of this—they explode everything: our church, our home, our neighborhood, everything. They kill *people* for this reason! They even try kill Dauod!" She shakes her head again and clucks her tongue in disgust. "So we have to go, yanni. Leave our home, after living there whole life. Leaving your home like this—it's like leaving a piece of you."

I look over at Daoud again. He is still wringing his hands, but now also silently crying as he looks out the window staring at nothing; the children have gone home. There is no one out there. I wonder what he sees—this poor old, diabetic, destitute half-blind man crying into his past.

"We just hope to feel safe again, Insha'Allah," Saleema's voice draws me back in, "to know our destiny." She then turns and notices her husband. She pauses, and then perfectly on cue, takes his hand in hers. They look at each other a moment, holding the other alive. That seems extreme, but sadly accurate. Then she looks back at me, tears having now filled her eyes; the pain now evident. I shake my head.

"Thanks for you!" she pushes through the tears. "I am sorry not offer you tea. We have no…" she starts to repeat herself. "But please know, in our hearts, you are now family." With these last words she touches her hand to her heart. Family. And she means it.

"Shukran," I respond. She now considers me family. Damn. Something tears at me on the inside. It tears deep.

This is the difference between our two countries: mine invaded hers and caused untold devastation and after a half hour of simply sitting in the same room together, she considers me family. I'm not sure if Americans would act the same were the situation reversed. As a matter of fact, I'm pretty sure we wouldn't.

We chat a bit more, exchanging pleasantries. After asking my age, she asks why I am not married yet with children. Back off old broad! This cuts a little close though, as it is something I ask myself with some regularity. Why aren't I married? Why haven't I found someone? But I just smile and shrug my shoulders, brushing off the question. In the words of a Magic 8 ball: *reply hazy*.

I like this woman a lot, even after she basically called me a spinster, but it is Dauod who has stolen my heart— Daoud with his silence and his handwringing, Daoud saying so much without saying a word. I am learning how proud Iraqi men are. They are historically a proud, strong people. So what must it be like to have fallen this far, and be able to do nothing about it? That is what breaks my heart: the sheer impotence of this man and all men here, really. There is nothing he can do to care for his family, retrieve his daughter or return his wife to their previous life. Nothing. He can't even serve me tea.

As we stand, about to leave, exchanging our 'shukrans' and 'ma'asalaamas,' Saleema hugs me and whispers desperately in my ear, "I only wish to see my daughter. Can you help?" I just look at her, for I can do no such thing. I wish I could.

*   *   *

"What are your dreams for the future?" I ask the translator to translate to the four Iraqi children in front of me. They all look at me blankly. So blankly it kinda throws me.

We are in a classroom at the Beirut Center for Women and Children. So it is a surprise when a father and his children walk in the classroom to get interviewed by the visiting Americans. I wonder if they have no mother.

"What do you want to be when you grow up?" I try again. No response. Nothing. Nada. Hm. I can't get them to say anything. Too much trauma perhaps?

Upon further questioning, I discover their mother is missing. Called it! I victoriously and pathetically think.

She has been kidnapped or ran away or was killed or something. I can't seem to get a straight answer, just vacant faces and rambling stories. I can't tell if it's the translation or something else. Am I missing something? As for my dream question, they still haven't answered that.

I don't relent.

It becomes irrationally important to me. "Do you have any *wish* for your future?" (I think maybe another word will help.) Nope. They just look at me as if I am an alien from another planet, which in many ways I am.

As the father unemotionally tells us his story of how close they have all come to death these past months, I finally get it. It is as though a dream for the future is impractical, foolish even. They would never presume to have dreams because quite possibly, they will not *have* a future, let alone a choice in it. So here they are—blank, drifting and motherless—children who do not dare to dream.

*   *   *

"Look! Empty! Look here. Nothing in cupboard! We have no plates, no cups, no food. We have nothing. Look!" The young Iraqi man emphatically declares as he gestures all around his barren kitchen, his wife lingering in the doorway.

We are here to talk to him and his family, but first he insisted on this fruitless tour. The kitchen is awful—dirty, moldy, empty and awful. I don't want to be in here anymore. I feel sick. This is their life everyday and it isn't right.

"Empty! Look!" he emphasizes again, as he opens the door of their run down refrigerator. Indeed. Two onions and an old potato is all they seem to have for this family of five.

Finally, the aid woman from the local agency we are working with calms him down and encourages him back into the living room, assuring us all that she will have someone drop off food to him soon. I look at his face. He looks at mine. I see fear and desperation...or is it simple surrender? I wonder what he sees.

*   *   *

Today we're interviewing all women. Their stories are so eerily similar: the woman leaves Iraq with her husband (if he's alive) and children (if they're alive) with no possessions (except what they could carry in the night across the border). They are currently living in limbo here—no past to remember, no present to speak of and no future to imagine. Their life's a lost cause. They only hope for a future for their children. Doesn't seem to me like too much to ask.

"Yanni, I have given up for me. I do not care about me, but my children. I wish for my children, yanni, to go to school, to be safe, to have a future. There is no hope for me now. I only hope for my children," a woman named Salman shares.

And then in walks Sawssan. Something about her stands out to me. She has a certain faded beauty about her, and sadness of course. Like the others, she has sadness.

As we get settled in, she sips her tea and makes a squinty face. I look at her questioningly.

"Not like in Baghdad," she says, through the translator, with a nostalgic smile, "I miss my mother's tea." Amidst her messy life, what a sweet, simple thing to miss—her mother's tea.

"My story? How do I know what to say? I am afraid to tell my story." But after a pause, she begins. "My husband's brother was shot in the head and killed in car my husband drive. The other bullets fired missed my husband's head by inches. He came home covered in his dead brother's blood and brains. Yanni, my husband in very big danger in Iraq. Because of this, my son who is six does not talk. I have only one son and now he does not speak. Is that good place to start?"

We are blown away. Yes, that is a good place to start.

"How is living in Beirut going?" I ask through the translator.

"It's yanni, how you say...humid in our room—not healthy. Not good for my husband's health. He has yanni, asthma. My husband, he sometimes works at a flower shop at night, sweeping floor. He is how you say...depressed? He was mechanical engineer in Iraq. Now...now he is just sick—asthma and yanni, hyperteension, doctor say. He should not have stress. It raise his blood pressure. But there is always stress. What we do? We need money. Yanni, what we do?" Sawssan nervously sips more of her tea and looks out the window.

We are all silent for several moments and then because I don't know what else to do, I ask another question. I'm always asking questions, asking for stories.

"Can you tell us why you left Iraq, Sawssan?" I notice the social worker in the room looking away, almost trying to escape. How many stories like this has she had to hear day after day?

Sawssan continues, "In Iraq, every time we go out, bombings. Youssef, my son, was so scared, yanni. We all were. So we stop going out. We just stay inside, yanni. My husband, he try to work, because he need to, but because we are Christian and because my husband drove for U.S., he would receive threats on the street. People say things. People threaten him and Youssef and me. They all wear black and hide their faces. Militia. And they would beat him and say things—they would say 'traitor'…'you work for U.S. government'… 'You leave or we kill you'."

I take a small sip of my tea. Screwed because they helped America—common story.

"So you left?"

"In the beginning," Sawssan explains, "we have no money to leave and no answer from America, so we have no choice but to live with these threats. For three years, we live with threats. Long time. Three years."

"Then what happened?"

"At last we borrow money and come here—to Lebanon. It's like a prison here, though. Just like in Iraq. I'm too afraid to go out or yanni, to allow my son to go out. So here too, we stay inside all day, every day. I'm very afraid for my son. He does not talk. I have only one child and he cannot talk. He just stop speaking, yanni…just stop. The doctor say I should get him back in school and see if he start speaking then, yanni. But what school? And that would mean letting him out of our room. I am too afraid." I sigh and she continues. "We never leave the room, only when we must, like today, to get food."

"And so, where is Youssef now?" I foolishly ask.

"At home in his room, with my husband. He just plays on the yanni, computer all day that we bring from Iraq. He always afraid. I know that's my fault. I know it is. But I..." she breaks here, about to cry. "Our situation cannot continue like this," and then making what seems like a brand new heartbreaking discovery says, "We only move from one prison to another."

"Sawssan, I'm so sorry. I know it doesn't help, but I'm so sorry." I hand her a tissue, thinking about Youssef stuck in his self-imposed prison of silence and internet games.

She continues, "Can I tell you? My son says a prayer every night. It's the only time he speaks, at night, to sing a prayer." And she begins to recite it in Arabic and then before I know it she is crying—full on, deep weeping, weight-of-the-world tears, for her son. At six years old, the only thing he can now safely offer the world is a prayer. God help us all.

=====================================
KIM'S ARABIC DICTIONARY second installment:
Min fadleek/ Please
La/ No
Chai/ Tea, incessantly offered
=====================================

I am standing with Shukraan. I know. I know. You're confused. I already told you shukran means "thank you". Let me explain: Her parents named this sweet girl

Shukraan because of her difficult birth. When they thought they were going to lose her in childbirth and didn't, in gratitude, they named her *thank you*. Beautiful.

And Shukraan won't let go of my...what's the word? Hand. Hand! What is wrong with me? I forgot the word hand! I remember every story but am losing my own memory. "No memory, only sadness." I am reminded of Saleema's words. Stop. I put it out of my head. Hand, hand. Shukraan is holding my *hand* so tightly, looking up at me. What must she think of me? This...American. What's my story?

I like this little girl. We have become some version of friends.

Their house is nice—homey, actually. It's nice to see. I really like this family. They're kind and putting on a brave face for me. They're also making me tea. More damn tea.

Shukraan still has my hand and wants my attention. She is trying to show me around her house. I let her pull me from this room to the next. Decorations, knick-knacks, toys, paintings on all the walls. The whole family makes art, I guess. Cool. This is nice. Four rooms in all...for six family members: Kitchen, living room, studio/bedroom, and bath. Her father was a professional artist and in his studio, he shows me his workbench.

"I do not make much anymore," he discloses. Brushes stand in a jar untouched. Naked canvasses lie on each other stacked and gathering dust. A few moments later, he shows me a small orange plastic engraving he did months ago. It says: "He who humbles himself, God rewards," I am told. It is interesting to me that these are the words he would choose. Humility before God. Even after everything he has been through. But it is my favorite color and I immediately love it.

"I want to give it to you," the father says, sensing my attachment to it.

"No, no, La. I can't take such a gift."

"Please," he insists. "For you. Min fadleek."

"Well then, may I buy it please from you?" I ask. I can't take this man's art for free. He has so little.

"No, you are family. It is a gift."

Family again.

I don't know what to do. I feel bad. I wish I hadn't looked at it so longingly. But after a few more minutes of cajoling, out of respect, I agree. I take the small orange Arabic-engraved gift, smile and say "Shukran," then look down at Shukraan still at my side.

I have to find a way to give him some money for this. I rack my brain trying to remember what cash I have on me. I think I have twenty dollars U.S. I can leave it here on the sly. But before I can check, Shukraan pulls me to the living room again. She starts pointing out paintings. She is getting excited to show me one of hers. Turns out she paints too, in her father's shadow.

Shukraan brings me back to the present with a squeeze of my hand. She points at a painting she made. I look at the painting, holding her hand.

Oh God.

Shukraan's painting is bloody and frightening. It is a child with her arms extended out like on a cross, gunshot wounds in both wrists with dripping blood and a huge gash in the head. It is heartbreaking and terrifying and something a child should never, ever paint, let alone experience. But this *has* been her experience, so this is what she paints. She looks up at me for affirmation, smiling.

"Shukran!" I say to Shukraan, while squeezing her sweet hand in one hand and my orange art in the other.

* * *

Najah serves us *candy* with our tea. I'm so excited. I'm craving a sweet. If only it was an éclair. This is nice though; a new accompaniment to the same ol' tea for a change. I wish the stories would change.

As I'm sucking diligently on my Iraqi sweet, Najah is telling me how her Iraqi husband used to beat her day after day until he finally left her to go back to Iraq—left her here in Syria with four children, alone. Lovely story. I swallow the end of the candy.

This is quite a small apartment to raise four children. Tiny. Only two rooms it seems. I look out the window at the street where her children are playing, seeking refuge from their refuge. I should have saved the candy and given it to them.

"I get $300 a month! How can I support my family on that?" Najah says through the translators. "But what choice we have to leave? Many of my friends had their children killed in Iraq. We have to leave. What choice is there?"

Najah goes on to describe just how many families in her neighborhood had their children kidnapped. The family would work very hard, begging and borrowing, to collect the demanded ransom and then the kidnappers would deliver a dead child to their doorstep anyway—a dead child to their doorstep. I can't even imagine.

"What choice I have?" she repeats.

I ask Najah about the possibility of resettlement.

"I cannot be resettled because although my husband leave me, he is still my husband. Iraqi law not permit me to leave without him or his signature saying it ok. But where is he? How I know? How I get him to sign divorce? So here we sit. No money, no food, no husband, no father, no future. Nothing."

I look at this woman. She's beautiful, or she used to be. She looks tired now, worn and sad. Her eyes look so sad. She continues, "My children say: do not worry about feeding us, momma. We are already dead."

I allow the weight of those last words to sink in. What child says those words? I guess a child as tired, worn and sad as their mother, a child who feels just as abandoned. Still, what child says those words?

"Do you blame America?" I ask.

She looks annoyed once my question is translated.

"This is not about America. I don't care about America! This is about *us*. Please, fix it! Help us!" Now I feel selfish and self-centered to have even asked.

And if that's not enough, she goes on to talk about her brother in Iraq whose throat was slit and her rent that just doubled and her father who needs open-heart surgery but no one can afford to pay for it so he will probably die. I wonder if I could pay for the surgery. All of this devastates me, of course, to the core, but I can't stop looking at the children on the street who no longer request food because they are already dead.

*   *   *

The food just got delivered to our table and holy crap: that is a *lot* of food. We ordered too much. My colleagues and I are out at a very nice traditional Middle Eastern restaurant to eat at the end of another very long day. This restaurant is quite nice. It feels like we are in a beautiful garden. Vines and flowers grow everywhere and romantic lights are strung up on tall trees. We also have a ridiculous amount of food. I can tell by the silence that descends as the food arrives, and the deeper silence that follows as we eat it, that we all recognize the fact.

We spend all day every day with people who basically have nothing and then tonight we find ourselves gorging on more food than we could ever eat. It was an accidental over-ordering to be fair, but still, the injustice hits hard. We eat the rest of the meal in continued silence, guilt overwhelming any other flavor we could taste.

*   *   *

Flies are buzzing everywhere. I keep swatting them away, but it seems to make no difference. We are sitting on the floor of a three-bedroom apartment. I notice none of the family makes any swatting motions. Huh. They have as many flies buzzing around and landing on them as I do, yet not one of them bothers to swat away any flies. That simple omission makes me wonder: why are they not swatting them away? Maybe they are just too tired—too tired of it *all*.

They apologize for having no furniture. We say it doesn't matter. They *keep* apologizing for having no furniture. We keep saying it doesn't matter; we are comfortable on the floor. They know we are not. They keep apologizing. The flies keep buzzing. Damnit! The flies are really bad. Are they always this bad?

The family looks destitute. They are dirty. The apartment is dirty. The floor is dirty. Everything is dirty. I'm listening to them tell their story, but I can't get over how many flies there are in here and how dirty it is. I don't mean to get all first-world on you here, but this is insane. I can barely concentrate, as I try to count the quantity of bugs and flies I see in my line of vision alone.

There have to be at least thirty flies on and around the baby's head. It takes everything in my power not to crawl over there and swat them away from her myself.

So basically this family has nothing, lives in filth, feels bad we have to sit on the floor and copes with a massive amount of flies every day. End of story.

The son, a quiet boy, who I learn is twelve, sits in the corner of our group near his family. He looks tired. I ask him if he is in school.

"La," Amir quietly says. He is not in school. The father ashamedly admits, "He must work. My son is the only one who can work. He supports his family." There might have been a note of pride in that last comment, but his head drops in shame.

I look at Amir. *He* supports this whole family. But for now he just looks at the ground. "What do you do, Amir?" We learn he works at a printing press over hot printing machines where the owners occasionally beat him. Yup. And he's twelve. Put that in your pipe and smoke it. But before you get your child labor abuse feathers all in a kerfluffle, remember Amir is probably the only one who can provide for his family. An Iraqi man working is basically illegal here. So even if Amir's job sucks *and* he is getting beaten, he can't quit. His family needs him— literally, to survive.

I look at this family through the wall of flies. Broken faces, every last one of them, even the fly-ridden baby— tired, broken faces. I wonder how much longer they can all sustain this.

*   *   *

"How did this happen? This is not my life. This is zero. This is like life fell down from a tree," Shefaa, a seemingly single woman in her forties, discloses in tears, with her young daughter in earshot. I keep looking at the girl—she seems unaffected.

"I try to kill myself two times. I have no reason to live."

Again, child within earshot! Again, child unaffected. Oblivious of my concern and seemingly her daughter's presence during this vivid tale, the mother continues, through the interpreter, to speak.

"Extremists kill my mother—kidnap her and kill her. Then one day, this militia—they come for me. They beat me on my way to university where I teach because I am not wear hijab, they tell me. I never wear hijab! My mother not wear hijab, too. But this does not matter. She was killed too. They say: You are too western and need to be taught lesson. They kick me and beat me many time. They punch me and kick me in the stomach. I fall over and they keep punch and kick. Now you will learn, they say! Now you will learn. I not understand these men. Their head is praying and their hand is killing. I was five months pregnant. Twins. In this time, I lose my babies, my mother and because of this, my God. I lose everything. Everything!" Shefaa ends her story in angry tears.

I watch the little girl on the floor. She is maybe eight or nine years old and is drawing. This whole time, she just keeps drawing. I watch her reaction. She seems to have none. Has she been listening? Is she ignoring? Does she already know this story?

I wonder if the little girl wants to say, "You didn't lose me, mommy." But she doesn't. I wonder when she became numb to this story.

Magazine photographs of people modeling hairstyles cover the walls of their one-room fourth floor walkup apartment—hair in a bun, hair off to one side, blonde hair, black hair, curly hair, man hair. Shefaa must have been a hairstylist and keeps these around to remind her of her past, who she was. That's the only explanation I can make for this choice of décor.

"No, they are to cover the holes in the walls," she reveals when I ask, as she refills my teacup. "This apartment was terrible when we moved in, big holes in all the walls. These magazine photos were all we could think to do to cover up the holes."

I scoot in a bit closer to the little girl. She smiles at me. I notice she has pretty hair. I wonder if she styled it after one of the magazine photos.

I sip more of my tea while dusk falls.

*　　*　　*

We have just finished the 619th interview of the day. Well, maybe not the 619th, probably…the fifth. But it feels like 619. The stories are all the same: death, dismemberment, kidnappings, killings, terror and tears all accompanied by tea. Different faces, same stories; add tea.

As I walk down these old Beirut streets, I feel heavy, furious with the futility of this whole situation. These kind Iraqis sit here in their never-ending misery, with nothing to do but share their stories with visiting internationals hoping it brings about some change—any change.

As we turn the corner, five or six Iraqi teen boys see us and start running towards us. We have become famous in the neighborhood today: the American group going into homes and talking to all the Iraqis. Curiosity has been piqued.

"America! America!" one of the boys, maybe fourteen years old, shouts at me. The others laugh. I look at them all and smile, uncertain as to the intent. "We love America!" the others laugh and say something to each other in Arabic. I sense sarcasm, but I can't be certain. I laugh and wave at them. They all laugh and wave and run around chanting "America, America! Take us to America!"

"Take us with you. Save us America girl!" one of them yells to me, half-laughing. Save us. Huh.

I don't know what to think of this. I think they mean it but yet they're laughing at the impossibility of it. They're half-joking. But something tells me they would come in a heartbeat. The irony is they don't even *know* America. All they know is that we invaded their country and now things suck for them. They think our country is rich and that anything is possible there. But they don't know what they're asking. Not really. They're just trying to get out of their current Hell. They want out of this place where they are not welcome, where they can't attend school, where their parents can't work, where they are poor, and where they are without all the 'things' they left in their middle class homes.

See, this is an urban refugee crisis. These are urban refugees. In Iraq, they were middle class: lived in middle class homes, had middle class cars, middle class jobs, went to middle class schools and now… now they are often very poor and have very little, having had to abandon their middle class homes and middle class cars, often in the middle of the night, taking only what they could carry to escape with their lives. Squatters, often militias and other extremists like Al-Qaeda, now live in their homes. Due to death threats, accessing their bank accounts becomes a dangerous, if not deadly task. Even the money sent from family and friends still living in Iraq eventually dries up, as the Iraqi economy has been brutally slow to recover. There's truly nothing left at home. This is the status of things. And for most, it isn't new. Their dire situation has been going on for years. It's been six years since the invasion that initially started the refugee crisis. Six years is a long time to be stateless and homeless and all but forgotten.

The hardest thing for me is seeing the children. So many children in the streets—selling cigarettes, batteries, bread, anything to provide for their destitute families, instead of being in school. I learned that several countries hosting refugees are not signatories to the 1967 *Protocol Relating to the Status of Refugees*. Basically what that means is that there is no right-to-work for the refugees— refugees aren't allowed to work. It's actually illegal for the adult men to work, even cause for deportation. This is why so many children are forced to forgo school, most often begrudgingly by their parents, to try to get a job in a factory or on the street selling the odd cigarette or whatever they can get their small little hands on to support their family, all the while fantasizing about a place called America, where all their dreams can come true.

I smile at the boys as they jubilantly shout, "America!" amongst the Arabic.

* * *

I can't stop crying. I am sitting in the second row of the van, looking out my window at the streets of Beirut passing me by. We are on our way to the next family, the next story. What are we supposed to do? Short of giving them all my money, I don't know *how* to help. I don't know what to do.

We have created this refugee crisis by our invasion of Iraq. The ensuing violence, chaos and bloodshed created in the vacuum of power after our invasion of that country is *our* fault. We have to own that. I am not trying to be political here. I'm trying to be honest. I know we Americans would like to forget about Iraq, but we can't. There are two million refugees and another two million internally displaced and without us, none of them would be here. End of story. Now whether it's because of the shocking lack of press coverage for this humanitarian crisis or the flag-encrusted blinders we put on after 9/11, or both—the result is the same: astounding amounts of damage done in our name. This trip has been a wake up call for me. I know there is no appetite anymore, not that there ever was, for Iraq or its problems. But our shared lack of interest, knowledge or engagement does not make the problem go away, it only inflames it.

Was Saddam bad? Yes.

Are there bad Iraqis? Of course.

Did this country have problems before our invasion? Certainly.

But are we responsible for most of them in the last fifty years? Yes. (See also: sanctions, oil, Bush Senior, Desert Storm.)

In so many ways, for so many years, for so many misguided reasons, we have devastated this country and this region; yet assume no responsibility for the innocent victims of the devastation. While I am here, I meet these victims every day, guilty of nothing but being Iraqi. If only every American could do the same: meet an Iraqi. Or for that matter, an Afghani or a Pakistani!

I heard a saying once: *An enemy is only a friend whose story you haven't heard yet.* If only people could hear these stories. If only there were less drones, less xenophobia, less assumptions. If only you could *meet* the person you think is your enemy. Maybe then things would change.

I turn even further from the others in the van to face the dusty window, risking neck crampage for some simple privacy. I look out at the faces on the street in Beirut, wondering who else might be in refuge, trying to slip into oblivion, hoping not to be noticed. But then I feel a friendly hand on my shoulder attempting comfort. It startles me— it's Megan, of course. My colleague Megan has become a good friend on this trip. She is younger than me, but mature beyond her twenty-something years; and is truly just as devastated as I am by these stories. But her hand does nothing to ease the pain, much like for the refugees— listening to their stories does nothing to ease *their* pain. It only serves to intensify it. So because I can, I cry and cry as the city flies by.

What have we done?

```
=======================================
```
KIM'S ARABIC DICTIONARY third installment:
Na'am/ Yes
Dabke/ Traditional Iraqi dance
Boosh/ George W. Bush, former U.S. president
```
=======================================
```

"More tea?"

"Shukran!"

"We Iraqi make good tea, la??"

"Na'am!"

So. Much. Tea.

The man offering it this time is Hatm. He is my new favorite person in the world. What a joyful Iraqi man. In fact, I'm kinda crushing on this rotund, middle-aged man, heaving from the exertion. He just finished teaching me the Dabke.

"Is this Iraqi?" I ask, wanting to be sure I get the real deal cultural lesson here.

"Very Iraqi!" He claims and we laugh, exhaustedly sitting.

"Ahh, I don't hate Americans," he continues. "No one does. Iraqi people love American people. Now Boosh...? Eh." Somehow through all this tragedy, he has not lost his humor. He is a breath of fresh air.

"Obama? Obama very good. Boosh...like Hitler. Look around. *This* is Boosh Democracy!" Hatm gestures to his sparse apartment, far away from his real home. "Before withdrawing, please—find a suitable president for Iraq, one who is secular, and who drinks alcohol. Any religion will do."

This guy's a hoot! Any religion will do? Indeed, most Iraqis are surprisingly secular. We are led to believe they are all extreme Muslims. But Iraq is or was, a very modern and secular society—Sunni, Shia, Christians and others lived in harmony—until recently when all that changed with the invasion.

"You like your tea? Yes? We Iraqis, we make good tea, la?" Yes, yes, tea, Iraqi, yes. Sigh.

Hatm sticks his hands down his pants where he keeps them for almost the entire interview—another reason to like him. He then sits in the regionally required plastic patio chair. His happens to be white.

"Looking backwards...I didn't mind Saddam!" Wait, what? He stops, noticing my skeptical expression. "I mean, he was terrible dictator and we all hated him, but it was better than this. We knew how to live under him. But then after U.S. invasion...you destroyed my neighborhood! Suddenly, religion become important!" One hand comes out of his pants to gesture emphatically. "My neighbor was Christian. I am Muslim. So what? But yanni, things change. My wife never wore the hijab; then suddenly she had to or she would be killed. My neighbor Boris, his ten-year-old son was kidnapped, held for ransom, and then killed anyway. It does not matter your religion. There is someone to kill everyone in Iraq. This is Boosh democracy!"

I am learning so much: the history, the politics, the way to subtly play with your junk in your pants.

"And now my children, they won't have Iraqi citizenship. They don't even have *Lebanese* citizenship. They have nothing. What do I give them? Sometimes I wonder...you had educated people in Iraq, you know and they all leave! Now you leave Iraq to the uneducated and ignorant—Iraq!"

He guts me with this last line. I never thought about this before. Who are we leaving Iraq to? All the scholars, students, and professionals have left! It's too dangerous. They were the ones targeted because people who use their brains are a threat to those who don't. So along with a few who couldn't afford to leave and a few who chose not to, for whatever reason, the only ones left in charge are the extremists.

"I will never go back," Hatm continues. "There is no hope for things to return the way they were." He pauses. I have heard this from so many Iraqis. "So, here we are. I am putting my hopes in that things here will be changed," he says hopefully. "We sit every day here, thinking, waiting. We wait every day for change. Americans will bring change. Insha'Allah."

Insha'Allah. I'm told you say that when there is something you want to happen, but suspect it won't.

======================================
KIM'S ARABIC DICTIONARY fourth installment:
Hezbollah/ Political group designated as terrorist due to their terrorist-like activities
Shawarma/ Best sandwich in the world
Time [Eng.]/ Non-existent in Middle East
======================================

All of us American delegates are standing on a balcony overlooking the Mediterranean Sea, drinking our assorted teas and coffees waiting for the aid workers to meet us. Rough life, I know.

We were scheduled for a 9.30 a.m. meeting. It is now well past 11 a.m.—more evidence of the Arab non-compliance with the clock. People in this region are not as big on schedules as I am. I wish I could get to the point where it stops frustrating me. So far, I have failed.

Our group leader Vargas tells me to chill. "Drink some more tea and enjoy the view, Schultz!" So I try. But seriously—two hours late for a meeting? Who does that? I am secretly fuming, but trying to breathe. There are worse places to be stuck waiting, than on a balcony, overlooking this incredible valley. Lebanon is beautiful country, extraordinary really—mountains, valleys, sea. It has everything (including a bloody and tumultuous history of its own).

By midnight, (Okay, I might be exaggerating. It was a little after eleven a.m.) the aid workers finally arrive to the office (quite casually I might add). Then with no apologies but all of us quite well caffeinated, we're finally off. It's Hezbollah day! The day we go into Hezbollah territory. Sweet. My mom would freak out if she knew.

(P.S. Don't tell my very-nervous-for-her-daughter-in-the-Middle-East mom that I went to Hezbollah country. P.P.S. Hezbollah literally means the party of God: hizb-allah. Sounds super welcoming, right? God's party. Too bad it's not. P.P.P.S Who cares? Yippee! It's Hezbollah day. A day in crazy militia country.)

I love this. I love *everything* about this.

As we approach the border town of Tyr, in official Hezbollah territory, multitudes of multi-gunned militia men stand at the entry to the town, pointing their automatic rifles at us while examining the car and its participants. Holy guns Batman! (Or whatever the Arabic equivalent is.) Intense. At last, finding nothing worth shooting us over (heavy sigh of relief), we are allowed across the border aaaaaand…it looks pretty much like the other side. Disappointing. Hezbollah territory, you are very disappointing.

After the big stressful border crossing, we stop for lunch at a nearby outdoor café and have some of the best Shawarma I've ever had under the most watchful scrutiny I've ever felt. I can see Vargas is nervous.

"So, Vargas, why is everyone staring at us?" I casually ask.

"Well, we are clearly Americans. What business could we have here?" he reasons. "Of course, they will be watching us."

Huh. I decide to try to look less American. More casual. I know! I won't worry about time! I'll smoke! I'll...oh forget it. Clearly, I'm American. So I decide to just enjoy my shawarma and hope for the best, Insha'Allah. If it's my last meal, at least it's a good one. I love shawarma.

As we walk from the restaurant towards the van, I see a bucket of money on the ground with a woman standing over it. It appears to be charity. She looks very poor, and as I have some leftover coins in my pocket from lunch, I dig them out and go to drop them in the bucket.

"Oh, oh, Kim. Hold on. No, no, no." Vargas says, as he suddenly stops my arm, guiding me away. Vargas can read Arabic. "That *charity* sign says Hezbollah," he whispers with a smile, "you just about donated to a known terrorist organization!"

"Oh," I respond, looking back at the lady. She doesn't look like a terrorist.

"I'd have to turn you in to the U.S. government." He climbs into the van and now can't stop laughing. "You almost donated to Hezbollah. Classic! Well done, Schultz. Well done!"

I sigh and settle in. Shut up Vargas.

We finally make our way to a refugee home in Tyr and are sitting with a bunch of lovely Iraqi women. This particular family consists of a widowed woman, her widowed daughter, a crying infant and a widowed aunt. No men. All the men have been killed. The women fled Iraq before they were too. Smart move.

They seem pretty well off, truth be told. The place looks nice. They have pictures of some people on the wall, and knick-knacks on the furniture. This is rather fancy. They seem to be doing pretty good!

"Our neighbors help us," The older woman explains, with the baby still crying in the background. "Without them we would die. They are very kind to us." She looks somewhat nervously at the door.

I am warmed to hear this. Thank God for their kind neighbors, helping to feed and clothe these widowed women.

"We miss Iraq, yes, but it is better here. No shootings, no threats. We feel more comfortable here. We are happy," the daughter continues, glancing at her mother. Again, nice. Sure, they're not at home, they've lost all their family and possessions, but they are starting over and they seem mostly okay.

"Every week, a neighbor comes to us and brings money. They take good care. We miss Iraq of course, but we are happy." The mother smiles awkwardly and again she looks at the door.

Huh. What's going on? Every week someone comes and drops off money? Dang. Good neighbors here in Tyr!

But something feels a bit off. They seem equal parts nervous and a little too happy and Vargas seems a little too eager to get us out of there.

"Well, thank you so much for your time. Shukran! But we should go," Vargas says, as he stands up. I still have more questions to ask and am not quite ready to leave, but decide to follow his lead, sensing some strangeness.

As we say our "ma'asalaamas" and "shukrans", I look up and notice a picture of an Arab-looking fellow in full turban gear hanging above the door in a frame. Vargas discreetly gestures to the same picture as we leave.

"Famous martyr," he whispers, "Hezbollah is the 'neighbor' that takes care of them. Those folks are running this house and probably watching us right now. This isn't good. We need to go. Now."

Holy crap. Aforementioned Hezbollah (my favorite charity) finances their comfortable life here? This is gettin' good!

As we leave, with Vargas pulling my elbow, I look back at the women standing alone in the doorway, holding the crying little baby girl, and wonder what their future will hold. At least someone is taking care of them, I think. I just wonder what the price will be. We hurry into the van.

==
KIM'S ARABIC DICTIONARY fifth installment:
Asalaam Al-Ayakoum/ Traditional greeting, similar to
"hello"
Oud/ A traditional Middle Eastern guitar-like
instrument (See Omar/Kim meeting)
Dervish/ An energetic, whirling dance
====================================

It's almost dark, as I enter the basement of the community center—our end of the day meeting point—dreaming of my bed, a bath and a glass of wine. We are waiting for all of our colleagues to assemble before heading back to the hotel together. How do aid workers do this, every day? I honestly wonder.

There are a bunch of Iraqis hanging out and chatting together in a corner of the basement.

"Asalaam Al-Ayakoum," I offer, hoping for just a greeting in exchange, nothing else. Please God, no more stories. Let there be no more stories today. I try to smile as I sit down next to Megan, trusting she will tell me no tragic story. She smiles back, looking as tired as I feel.

There are both Iraqi women and men here, mostly sitting separately. Some women are in the headscarves. Some are not. All ages are present—from young, single, twenty-something men to older women. I take it all in. Iraq.

Then suddenly I hear drumming. Huh. Fun. Music could be good right now. An Iraqi man has grabbed a drum and then another grabs an oud and they are playing together. It's lovely and Iraqi and makes me happy. We start to smile and laugh and move—the Iraqis and the Americans. I start to loosen up. As there are no translators here, we can say very little to each other, but with music, we don't need to. So we dance, teaching each other our cultural moves, and laughing to see the other try them on. We are all enjoying ourselves—a surprisingly perfect end to the difficult day.

Before I know it, a longhaired, olive-skinned man with big, vacant eyes, in a bright blue shirt, whom I hadn't noticed before, has taken center stage. This man wants to dance! We all step aside and let him have the focus, as it seems that is what he wants. He is dancing joyfully, fully and with abandon. We are all laughing as he flirts with both the men and women, and begins to do a mock strip tease. This guy's a character!

"Oh yeaaaah!" we all shout. Someone yells, "Dance, baby!" But now, clothes really are coming off. Is he really gonna get naked? The energy shifts. No one knows what to do. Some are still catcalling, but the rest of us have sat back down. He has the stage. It's more than slightly awkward. He's half-naked dancing with an office wheelie chair, sending it spinning violently in every direction, with his arms gesturing wildly. I am beginning to feel dizzy…and uncomfortable. I look to my colleagues. They look as mystified as me. This is not a traditional dervish dance. This is not *any* kind of traditional dance. This is different. Something is happening. I look back at our dancer. The blue shirt is off and the pants are about to be. But this is no longer flirty or fun, it has turned fraught and frenetic. I feel scared for some reason because strangely, this dance now feels like…a battle, like war. I instantaneously start to cry. I don't know if it's the day or the dance, but I want him to stop. I want all of this to stop. I don't want any of it.

In his half undressed state, he comes up to each of us asking us to dance. He wants a partner. No one wants to be his partner. Everyone shakes their head no—la! As he approaches me with his arm extended in desperate invitation, I hesitate and almost say yes. I feel like he needs someone so badly and I want to help, but he scares me with his volatile emotions. That, plus he's almost naked. So I decline him like the others. *La. Sorry!*

We all watch in silence—awkward, apprehensive, melancholy silence—as he and the chair spin some more, sweat and his hair flying frantically, until at last he collapses. It's over. The drumming stops. Time suspends. The room is silent. No one moves. I can hear my heartbeat.

We all, Iraqis and Americans both, just look at him, holding our collective breath, uncertain what to do next.

At last, he stands back up, pauses and then he does the strangest thing: he bows. He actually bows, his apparent impromptu performance over. After a delayed moment, we quietly applaud, looking at each other. Then the blue shirt guy picks up his blue shirt and says to us in pretty decent English, "You made him appear, you know," and then walks out of the room. I'm pretty sure he is crying. As am I.

I want to go back to the hotel now.

*   *   *

A week into the trip and I'm sitting on the lobby couch of our swanky hotel in Amman, Jordan now drinking tea. It *is* swanky. Seems kind of unfair, considering what we are doing all day and with whom, but what can I do? I take another sip. I seem to only drink tea these days. Never drank so much tea in my whole damn life. But it's comforting somehow. Seems right. Although today it does nothing to soothe the emotions. The waiter across the lobby has noticed the odd tear fall down my cheek. He smiles at me gently.

We arrived here late last night from Lebanon, and will be spending a week here before moving onto Damascus.

Although we were only in Beirut a short time, I feel I have lived a lifetime. I met so many people and heard so many stories. I feel over-tired, overwhelmed and under-useful. We are so damn lucky as Americans and we don't even realize it. We live unaware of our geographically born-into luck. It's only the random taste of terror attacks we occasionally get that even come close to giving us a glimpse into how much of the world lives on a daily basis. We live so protected. *I* have lived so protected—even in New York. We are so damn lucky.

These Iraqis I meet have lived through so much and are willing to share it with me. They are willing to share their stories. How lucky am I. So my job is to simply listen.

The thoughtful waiter brings me more hot tea, chai as they say, and gives me another encouraging smile. I try to smile back.

*   *   *

It is a day off and I am in Petra. Historic, wonder-of-the-world, city-built-in-rock Petra. And surprise, surprise: it's hot. So I decide to invest in a camel ride since it's a pretty long walk on foot. I look at all the camel options and choose a nice-looking man across the entrance that happens to be looking at me. After negotiating price, I hop on (she says, as if it was that easy. Camel boarding is *not* easy. Try it sometime.)

After hanging on for dear life barely surviving the camel standing up part, we're off...slowly. Camels are slow. Very, very slow. And tall. I get quite a view from this height. I take the deepest breath I have in a week.

Petra is amazing, beautiful with it's rose-colored stones cut into the rock. It is sometimes called "Rose City" for that very reason. My camel guide, Aamir, is Bedouin— a tribe of traditionally nomadic desert dwellers. He is also chatty, giving me the low-down on Petra, including that whole Rose City business. His English is quite good. He apparently speaks six languages, learned from this job alone.

"I didn't go much to school. I always working here to support my family. I take camel for tourists since I was six. You must learn languages to get hired, to make tip," he smiles. "So I learn languages. English is easy. So many people speak English!"

I laugh.

"But my Russian? Not so good."

Impressive. My camel guide speaks more languages than I do.

I take a deep breath, looking around, feeling the sun on my head and the camel under my butt. I feel a bit like a princess. What luxury. If any of the Iraqis I have met so far came to Petra, I doubt they would hire a camel. Aamir looks at me and inquisitively smiles.

"You like camel, lady?"

"Yes," I respond.

"You like Jordan?"

"Sure. It's nice."

It seems I don't have very many words these days. This trip and this experience have taken a lot out of me already and we're not even half done. I'm not sure how mentally stable I feel today. I cried a lot last night. I could even cry now if I wanted. It's that easy these days. But I don't.

We ride a bit, with Aamir looking back at me occasionally. Lost in my thoughts, he startles me when he speaks again.

"I would like to marry you."

"I'm sorry?" I inanely respond. Did he just say he wanted to marry me?

"I think you are the most beautiful woman I have ever seen." (Clearly he lives a sheltered life.) "I would like to have you as wife. We will sleep in a cave, but I keep apartment in the city too, so do not worry. Every morning, I will bring you breakfast and coffee. Every night we watch the stars. It is a beautiful life. I take care of everything. You have to do nothing. And I will pay for you the price of one hundred camels."

Did I just get offered one hundred camels for my hand in marriage? I look at my camel man, actually considering the offer. I mean...stars every night and coffee every morning? Not too shabby...

"Well? What do you think? Marry me, lady? I am serious."

I like that he proposed calling me lady.

"My name is Kim," I offer to my would-be fiancé, trying to laugh it off, playing the whole thing off like it was a joke. Call me crazy, but the whole way back, I wondered what life would be like living in a cave with Aamir.

... and whether or not one hundred camels was a good price.

==
KIM'S ARABIC DICTIONARY sixth installment:
Yella/ Let's go
Haram/ Something taboo, forbidden in society
Beera/ Yes, you got it—beer!
==

Vargas and I are sneaking a beer. Yes, we are. We are sitting at a table outside in a public courtyard in Jordan and both of us have a brown-bagged bottle between our legs. Our Jordanian minder doesn't seem to mind, although he doesn't drink. We do, though—tonight anyway. We decided we needed beer. Our minder reluctantly agreed. I snag another sip from the rather obviously disguised bottle, catching Vargas' eye. We both laugh at the ludicrousness.

"It's come to this, eh Schultz?"

"Yup. It has. Proposals from camel drivers and forbidden alcohol. I'm so happy for this beer!" I shout a little too loudly. Vargas is cute. Too bad he's married.

"Please be careful," our minder reminds us. "Drinking is haram here. Is not safe if we are seen with beera, min fadleek." He looks over his shoulder again. Well the fun is gone now. I don't want to get the guy in trouble, or ya know, get stoned by an angry mob of Islamic fundamentalists.

Vargas and I nod in silent agreement. It's getting dark anyway. We each take one more clandestine sip and then he grabs both bottles throwing them in the nearby trash. I wince, but understand and agree. Still, I feel like I'm living in prohibition era! But this ain't no juice joint. And it's time to become a Middle East teetotaler once again.

"Yella," Vargas calls out, leading the way. We head back to the hotel, the sweet, sweet taste of alcohol on our breath.

```
=======================================
```
KIM'S ARABIC DICTIONARY seventh installment:
UNHCR/ United Nations High Commissioner for
        Refugees
Usra/ Family
Smoking [Eng.]/ Still a thing in the Middle East
```
=======================================
```

I have to get some air. I step into an alleyway behind the Refugee Center in Amman looking for a private moment. But there is a man on the far wall smoking and looking at me. I don't want to go to him, but I know I have to. This is my job. Talking to refugees is my job, even though I no longer want to. In a weird way, he seems to be almost *waiting* for me, this man. He keeps stealing glances. I relent. My self-declared break must wait.

I find a translator and start walking towards the back end of the alley where he is standing. We pass several men and smoke billows all around us. So accustomed to the anti-smoking policies in New York, I am always startled by the amount of smoke in the rest of the world. Do people really still smoke? Apparently they do, I must acknowledge as I walk through the haze.

This man looks at me without saying a word. He knows I am here with the American organization. Perhaps he thinks I can help him. I hope not. I don't want to disappoint him. We exchange partial smiles. He is younger than I initially thought, and he is crying, not full on crying, but the kind where the tears fill in your eyes like water balloons. It is the kind of crying which pulls your audience in, eagerly awaiting the first heavy drop to fall. This is how Raheel is crying. This is how I am pulled in. He tells me he doesn't know what he should do. He is desperate.

"My whole family is in U.S. in place called Iowa. But U.S. not take me. They say I twenty-three-year-old male. I adult. I need apply on my own. But that is not how it work here in Middle East. This is my family. Usra stay together. And now I alone." Raheel is now gently crying—that first laden tear falling into an aqueduct. I worry the dam will break. I have told him I can't help his case, but I know he still hopes I can.

"I know no one here. I so alone! I want go to Iowa!" I'm not sure an Iraqi man in Lebanon has ever spoken those last words. Or any man in Lebanon. Or any man for that matter! (Sorry Iowa...)

"Last week, UNHCR, they deny me. Why? Why?"

I stand listening, trying not to cry—my own dam threatening to break, as he rubs out his cigarette with his foot.

"They say I has bad leg, cannot go U.S. because of this. Is this America? What kind of America is this? Tell me." He looks at me waiting for my answer.

America and Iraq look very differently as to what constitutes family. America says, "You're eighteen? You're on your own. Adult." But Middle Eastern culture is very different. Family—usra—is family, old or young. And all ages stay together, until a new family is created through marriage. But Raheel was left behind and the tears are streaming down his face. He cannot stop them now. Damn. Dam.

The translator is then called away, so we stand alone, this crying man and I, looking at each other, both of us mute and impotent. He leans against the wall, turns modestly away, and starts to light a second cigarette. I breathe it all in—America and Iraq. Despite all the smoke and mirrors, here we are.

At his insistence, I finally take his name and case number and promise I will do what I can to help. But there's nothing I can do to help. Nothing.

*   *   *

"I lost both my brothers," Mona, a woman in her very early twenties, catatonically states from her kitchen table on a deep exhale. "One brother was killed when U.S. bombed his house. He was making dinner when U.S. bombed it. Accident they say."

She is so not here, I feel like she is *also* dead. It seems that even sitting in that blue plastic chair is hard for her— that she needs to be laying flat. Her bones look heavy with grief. I see and feel it all around her. It is palpable. This is her life now and it is clearly too much for her. It seems hard for her to even breathe. Perhaps she feels guilty she can?

Her elderly mother wearing a hijab sits in the corner looking down, avoiding eye contact, nervously playing with the scarf around her neck. These stories are never easy to retell. I wonder if it causes more pain than good to share this story with us. I reach out and play with the baby in the bassinet next to me. A tear streams down my cheek. What life do you have ahead of you, little one? Your family is obliterated.

"My other brother was shot in the head in street by U.S. Army while walking home. Also accident they say." Two brothers, both dead, both by the United States of America—be it by a miscalculation, misdirection or misjudgment. U.S.: 2. This family: 0.

"U.S. sent apology letter…for bombed house, not for brother shot in head. You wish to see the letter?"

We perfunctorily say yes. Why not? Show us the letter! The mother sits fingering her hijab, as the practically dead young woman pulls herself out of the plastic chair and looks for the apology from my country.

*   *   *

"Who asked for your help, America? Tell me!" the angry aid worker yells at us from behind the table in Amman— hot, loud Amman. My colleagues and I are right now standing in for an entire nation and there is nothing to do but listen. "People are worse off than before. Who asked you to come? Who died and made you God! Who gave you permission to do this to these people? You have ruined so much. Just go home."

Dang. But Laure has a right to be angry. She has been working helping Iraqis stranded here in Jordan for years. She has seen the situation deteriorate. She has seen Iraqis suffer and she has seen the west turn a blind eye to the damage they wrought. Her job is to clean up the mess we made.

My pulse is racing. I want to say, "I know! I agree! I'm sorry!" But I just sit and listen, allowing her to vent. Why am I being blamed for this? Maybe we are the first Americans she has had contact with since the invasion, or maybe every guest from the west gets this special welcome. The irony is she's not even Iraqi—she's Jordanian! It's not even her people. But they've *become* her people. And she's mad. And I can't blame her. She taps her pen on the conference table.

"What are the older people to do? They cannot work. They cannot provide for themselves. They have nothing left. This is how their life ends? And what about the young men? No one thinks of them. Yes, there are more vulnerable populations, but these young men have no future, no family and are very susceptible to extremists who promise them food and a roof over their head. Please don't forget about these young men. Tell your country. These young men are the future. They will also be your destruction. They are spinning in circles with no options. How do I tell these young men they will be the *last* ones to ever be helped? That they will be the *last* ones to leave!"

I am thirsty. I am tired. I am afraid. I wasn't expecting to be so deeply affected by this experience, to be completely changed by these people, by these stories. I wasn't expecting the story to demand so loudly to be told, for it all to be so relentless. I wasn't ready for this.

Okay, listen, I am well travelled, informed and educated. I know stuff. I don't think I'm ignorant or naïve or stupid. But I didn't know *any* of this. Why wasn't I *told* any of this? I didn't know this is what happened when we decided, unasked, to bring "freedom" to Iraq. I didn't know how many innocent people, having no connection to terrorists, 9/11 or weapons of mass destruction, lost a mother, uncle, husband, child, neighbor. I didn't know how many people were hurt and killed and kidnapped. I didn't know how very few options the Iraqis had for food, employment, education, future. I didn't know how thoroughly America screwed them lo these many years— and that's the ones we didn't *kill*! And this is saying *nothing* about the first Gulf war or the sanctions or... And these people I am meeting with are the supposed *lucky* ones—lucky to be alive! And yet most of them, I have been told, would rather be dead. It's easier, they say. I didn't know. God help me, I didn't know. And here I am being yelled at for my countries' ignorance, for my own. How can I deny her that?

But let me remind you, it's the Jordanian woman who is yelling at us—not an Iraqi. Never has an Iraqi yelled at me. Why aren't Iraqis yelling at me? This is what I don't understand. I know it's complicated—Saddam, which religious sect you belonged to, hopes for better lives with U.S. invasion, etc., etc. But still, it shocks me that as an American, how warmly I am welcomed. The Iraqis just quietly offer us their stories and their tea. But it is this Jordanian woman who works day in and day out with Iraqis in their non-stop misery—it's *she* who yells at us and who wakes me up to everything that is going on here. So I sit across from Laure leaning back in my office wheelie chair and listen, remembering for a moment the last time I saw a chair like this.

There is nothing else to do.

*   *   *

There was a child somewhere. In Damascus? Muhammad. I remember. His name was Muhammad. It was after I met Omar, I think.

"Will you tell me a story? Maybe a story from Iraq? Your favorite story?" I asked in some community center to one of the older girls hanging around. She looked at me demurely shaking her head no. So I asked the older boy and then the other girl.

"La, la," everyone said. They were shy. Please? Min fadleeck? No dice.

Until, listening to the funny American girl attempting their native language, the beautiful little dark-haired boy— the youngest, maybe six—finally broke down with a shy smile and agreed.

"Na'am," he said. He had a story.

I bent down to listen and then waited for the translator to translate.

"It's about a chicken and a cock."

Excellent! How Arab, I thought!

He continued. The translator paused and then declared: "The mother of the chicken died and then the chicken died." Well, I thought, there's a chipper chicken story.

"Do you have another story, Muhammad?" I remember asking. Muhammad nodded and smiled, thrilled with how well his first story went over.

This one is about two brothers who live on a farm. (So far so good!) The older brother took care of the younger one. (Nice.) Until the older brother got sick (uh-oh) aaaaaaand died, leaving the younger one all alone. And then as an additional kick in the gut, the young one died too.

Enough. My God, I can't breathe anymore. It doesn't matter who they are or where they are, the stories are all the same. And no one can save anyone.

But I'd be damned if I wasn't going to save Omar.

*   *   *

"Do you mind dropping me at the hotel first?" I ask Vargas as we finally leave smiling Sarah's apartment.

It's so hot in Damascus today. (Although honestly, it's hot in Damascus every day.) The Syrian sun is taking its toll on me. Sweat rolls down my temple. Dang it. I wanted to remain fresh today. I didn't want to sweat, not today.

"What, do you have a hot date or something?" Vargas asks.

Weeellll. I didn't want to tell Vargas. After all, he is in charge of this delegation and I don't want him to be conflicted over my newfound interest in one particular Iraqi, but I was late to meet Omar at our hotel and I was afraid Omar would leave. Professional conflicts be damned.

"Yes, as a matter of fact. And I am over an hour late!" I blurt out.

"Omar???" Vargas asks, having clearly caught wind of our brewing romance last night at the artist social hour. "Holy shit! Really?"

Vargas is cool, but still I decide to portray this as casual and low-key.

"Yes. I'm going to his studio to look at his paintings," I unswervingly announce.

"Omayyad!" he belts out, referencing the name of our hotel, as if saying "OhmyGod!" as we always do – our inside joke. His shoulders drop and he lets out a sigh, wiping some sweat, looking at me as though to say, "You are unbelievable!" I don't know if he's more annoyed with the heat or me. Well, I guess I do know. As hot as it is today, it's me. I know.

I defend myself, "An hour! I am an hour late. Sarah's interview was longer than we planned!" I hope the lax Middle Eastern time rule is in effect for pseudo-dates with Iraqis.

Vargas quips, "Well, at least you still have your priorities, Schultz." I make my own annoyed face at him. "Let's go. Yella!" he yells, smiling at me.

Come on. I think I really like this guy.

*   *   *

When I finally arrive back home at the Omayyad Hotel (OMY! Omayyad!), Omar is nowhere in sight. I blew it. I was too late. He's gone.

The Damascus Omayyad is another swanky hotel— nice enough to make any American feel comfortable and any refugee feel quite uncomfortable. There are fancy chandeliers and fancy tapestries and fancy furniture. Fancy, fancy, fancy.

Friendly English-speaking faces welcome the tourist, while unfriendly-looking hotel security guards against any possible non-English speaking troublemakers in the lobby, especially those who look Iraqi. The Syrian secret police are just a phone call away. Actually, they are probably already here in the lobby, behind that plant, looking at me.

For reals. Vargas said they have been following us all day. Syria is like that: secret police everywhere. I love it.

Crap. Omar must have left. I would have too if I were him. Too risky. After all, like everywhere else, Iraqi refugees are officially illegal here in Syria, eligible for dangerous deportation back to Iraq at any moment. Most state police turn a blind eye, but not all, and certainly not if you are "causing trouble" by sitting in a swanky, tourist hotel claiming to be waiting for your potential new American lovah. That's right—I said "potential lovah".

I wonder if I was too obvious last night. I mean, I was so quick to agree to meet him. "Yes," I chirped, "I would love to see your art!" I wish I had answered in a lower register—less chirpy. What must he think of me? American whore with a capital ho is what! Oh well, its done.

We were supposed to meet here at the hotel and go to his studio from here. Plan in action. Date in motion. Bingo. Until the damn reason I'm even in this country slowed me down. A pox on my job!

I stand helpless in the hotel lobby, desperate to remedy this. I need to find Omar. This isn't the end. This isn't how it ends.

Then I remember I have his number. Good Lord, he gave me his number last night! Hallelujah! All is not lost.

But how to make a call, how to make a call...

I practically run to the private phone booth thingy in the lobby, certain I can manage the Syrian phone system on sheer wit and adrenaline alone. I cannot. It's antiquated, in Arabic and beyond my pay scale.

I hustle back to the desk and after much finagling and finger-pointing and failed attempts in my barely-conversational Arabic (where is all the English speaking staff now?) the front desk staff eventually agree to help, though suspicious of why this American woman is calling an Iraqi male. (Hussy with a capital hu!)

I hand the sacred piece of paper with his name and number on it over to the man helping me. I feel the secret state police watching me. Are they on the staircase? Behind that column? Relax, Kim. They are probably simply sitting on the couch like everyone else watching the crazy American cause a scene.

Ring, ring. Ring, ring. (Syrian rings are funny. Sounds like I'm on a 1950's movie set or The Great Depression...or whenever they had funny rings.)

"Omar?"

He picked up! He picked up! Omayyad! He picked up.

"Kim? I am sorry. I waited for over one hour."

"I know. I'm so sorry. We got held up with this one woman who..."

"What you say? Talk slow please..." he reminds me.

"I said I'm sorry. We were so late. We just…"

"It's ok, I just couldn't stay lobby any…."

"I know. I'm sorry."

"I am still…"

"Could you …"

We are totally speaking over each other, which makes us both laugh. I am just so grateful to hear his voice.

"Maybe I come back?" Omar asks tentatively.

I breathe a giant sigh of relief. Yes, he was only blocks away. It was not too late. He would come back. He has to come back. After all, it was in the coffee grounds.

O.M.Y. I am going to see him again.

*   *   *

Well-played Omar. Well-played.

I am standing in his apartment slash studio. How convenient that we are looking at his art in his home. I should have seen that one coming. Although what did I expect? A separate Soho studio? I mean, come on: refugee. And in his defense, he has been nothing but a gentleman.

That is, after he made me take two buses and walk up a very big hill to get here. I mean, very big hill. I didn't want to be all Richy Rich and suggest a cab, but man, that was a hike! I didn't quite expect him to live so far from the hotel. Although again: refugee. Those neighborhoods are usually different from the fancy hotel neighborhoods.

And now, in his apartment-studio combo, the sane part of my brain starts to ask questions: What am I doing here? More importantly, what am I doing here alone? I never told Megan or Vargas exactly where we I was going, truth-be-told. What if he kills me or rapes me or who-knows-what-me!

Actually, I don't believe any of that is possible. It's Omar. For some unknown reason, I trust this "Omar". I feel connected to him. Although that's possibly what murder victims might say to themselves before they're murdered by a guy they really felt "connected" too. Sorry. I'm from New York; these thoughts come up. Especially after ten years in the big city. Ten years of single-hood. Ten years of sporadic dating and constant disappointment. And yes, ten years of hoping not to be murdered over a latte by a lunatic. And yet, here I am in a strange man's apartment in a foreign city. Perhaps not my smartest move.

Perhaps he is also nervous, as we both seem slightly stilted and clumsy as we walk around slowly looking at his art, each of us unsure where or when or how to move. He feels it too. I know he does. We can barely look at each other. Possibility of murder aside, it's very exciting. My heart races and my breath seems not enough. Just look at his paintings, Kim. Focus on his paintings: They are beautiful. He can paint. Thank God the man can paint. I love them instantly—bright, suggestive, aching, plaintive, rich and racy. Yes, a little racy…boobs! Lots of boobs in his work. Boobs. Boobs. Boobs. Clearly, he's not a conservative Muslim. Double yay! Because the best news? I have boobs!

I suddenly notice him standing close behind me, very close. Very, very, very close. I feel the energy zip, zip, zipping between us. Yow! I decide to pretend to look at more art—safer that way. Art! Look at all the art. All the while all I am really doing is feeling how close we can get without it being inappropriate. It's a fine line: arms almost touching, my hair brushing his shoulder, gentle hand sweep. Or is it? This might all be in my imagination. I have a vivid imagination. I am an artist after all.

I mean, maybe this is just more Middle Eastern hospitality. As I have mentioned: Iraqi people are very hospitable. Plus, I really don't know just how Muslim he truly is. I mean 'boobs on canvas' yes, but real boobs? I don't know. Maybe my behavior is haram. Maybe I'm offending him. I just don't know. I don't have a Magic 8 ball. I mean, me just being here alone with him is probably haram in most conservative circles. But he doesn't seem bothered. I'm equal parts confused and titillated.

Nonetheless we dance our second ceremonial dance a few moments longer—a few more luscious, lingering moments. Omar leads. I decide to quit seeking an answer (*ask again later*) and instead follow, allowing myself to be suspended in the time warp in which I find myself—the misty, magical, sensual suspension of time, in an old-world country with my old-world Omar.

At last Omar breaks the magic, stepping out of our magnetic field and stepping back from me. I catch my breath, almost stumbling from the loss of him. I look at him, mouth ajar, senses activated.

"A beer, maybe?" he asks. I release my breath.

Are you kidding? This is a dream! He paints like this, he flirts like this and he has beer for me! Yes! Yes! Yes!

"Sure, that'd be fine," I answer casually, trying not to seem too excited about a beer.

Once Omar steps into the kitchen to retrieve our beers, I begin my investigation. Who is this guy?

I start to wander around his place. He has three bedrooms. Dang. More than I have. Oh, and he has a laptop. Good. But he only has a hotplate. Bad. He has a balcony. Good! Wait, what? Balcony? Really good. But his couch is broken. Bad. He's humming a ditty. Good. Cute actually. I'm quite charmed for a moment. No. No time for charm. Back to work. He has no shower curtain. Bad.

Well...wait, no, that's just strange. Why does he have no shower curtain? That's weird. Is that Arab? How does water not go everywhere? Wouldn't the floor get all wet? How does the floor not get all wet? But before I can finish my shower curtain query, Omar is behind me, watching me. I can feel his presence.

Busted, I turn.

"I like your bathroom!" I chirp a little too happily, and a little too loudly.

Omar smiles. He doesn't seem to notice or mind.

I spy beer on a tray and quickly pick it up; I hold it and say "Cheers!" What is the equivalent to 'cheers' in Arabic, I wonder? Aw, hell! Who cares? Beer! I've got beer. Hello my old friend. I have missed you in this alcohol-is-not-very-prevalent-part-of-the-world.

We drink one, then two glorious beers on that glorious balcony overlooking glorious Damascus. Talking, flirting, gazing into each other's eyes. It's like a dream. I like him. I really like him. And here's the kicker: I think he likes me too!

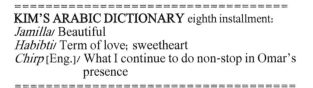

=================================
KIM'S ARABIC DICTIONARY eighth installment:
Jamilla/ Beautiful
Habibti/ Term of love; sweetheart
Chirp [Eng.]/ What I continue to do non-stop in Omar's
      presence
=================================

It's dark out now. We're standing on his balcony overlooking the now twinkling blue lights of Damascus below. They look like stars.

"Nejoom," Omar says. "Nejoom?" I ask. "Nejoom," he answers. Stars. I look at the twinkling city lights once again. Perfectly lost in both the blue lights and his brown eyes, I listen to his broken English: He travels back and forth to Baghdad regularly, sends money home when he can, considers himself more Western than Arab, watches American movies every night, has a best friend named Alaa, not Allah/God/Allah but Aha-laa, calls home every time there are bombings in Baghdad to make sure everyone is still alive and thinks I am jamilla. "Jamilla?" I ask. "Jamilla," he says. Beautiful. He thinks I'm beautiful.

We look at each other and are so close to kissing it hurts, but I decide to delay. I mean…I'm not even sure this is legal. Am I allowed to kiss a refugee on a mission to interview him? What would my sponsoring organization say? Could this in some way negate all the interviews I've done? Am I being ridiculous? Of course I am! Kiss him, Kim!! But why won't he kiss me? He should kiss me! OMY, this is so difficult! What is the right course of action in this situation? I'm not sure there is one! I'm not sure anyone anywhere in the history of the world has ever been in this situation before. Ever! So I pull back from Omar and simply smile.

Well played, I think. Well played.

He pauses, takes a swig of his beer and turns away. I sigh, from relief or disappointment, maybe both. The city lights below us pull my attention again, so we both watch the lights flicker in silence. I feel content here with him. And that thought makes me nervous. It's a crazy thought. I don't have time to feel content with him. I leave this country in less than a week! I don't have time for a relationship like this, if it even becomes a relationship. I mean...it's a ridiculous thing to even consider.

The seductive spell temporarily broken, I decide to go back inside to look at his paintings some more. I need to escape the extreme thoughts in my head and the extreme romance of this balcony. And perhaps now I can actually see the paintings, since I'm not quite as nervous as I was before. He follows me inside. I wander around a few paintings, still feeling the heat of our almost-kiss in every pore. I notice a beautiful, smiling woman who appears in several paintings. I ask him casually about her.

"So, who is that woman?" I say, not at all casually, sounding more like a stalker than I wanted.

"This girl live in Baghdad and I loved her" Jealousy overtakes me. I hate her and her casual, sexy smiles!

"But I never meet her," he finishes. Okay, jealousy subsides. Loved her but never met her? Wha-? Apparently, her father would not allow it after the invasion. Something Sunni/Shia. I wonder what he is. Sunni or Shia. I don't ask. Maybe I'm sick of asking questions. Maybe I no longer care.

So Omar would wait for this woman to leave her home every day so he could steal a glance of her as she walked across the street. Every day, he would just watch her (apparently I'm not the only stalker!), always careful as to never be caught as she would be punished if her father suspected Omar of stealing glances. Really? I mean fifty years ago sure, but today? This happens today? To the man I am head over sandals for? Where am I?

"Please. You want to sit?" Omar offers, gesturing to the sad, little couch. Sure, why not. I sit, already missing the romance of the balcony.

He asks me about my writing, my acting, and my family. I ask him about his painting, his life here, and his dreams. All the while, the woman in the painting on the wall hovers over us, stealing glances, as I try to find a comfortable spot on the broken couch. Sit still, Kim. Don't act like the couch is broken. You'll make him aware that you're aware that his couch is broken. He sits on a nearby chair, not on the couch by me. Strange. Respectful?

Strange. I tune back in and notice he is desperately trying to tell me something.

"Kim, I..." He moves his chair in closer.

He is struggling. He felt a connection immediately. Meeting was no accident. This was meant to be. But we are different. He thinks I think he is a Bedouin man, living in cave.

"No, no, Omar," I laugh in response, remembering my Bedouin proposal. "I don't think you are a Bedouin man!"

"Maybe later when my English is better, I can speak my heart better. It's just...I..."

"No, you're doing fine, Omar. Please. Say what you are saying," I lean forward, but now he's not looking at me. He's so nervous, attempting to speak his heart in his non-native tongue.

Finally, the broken words stop. He is done and simply looks at me, not knowing. And in one of the few times in my life, I look at him, knowing. And then...

...I kiss him, speaking my heart with my native tongue.

I kissed him because I knew he would never kiss me, could never kiss me first, for so many reasons. I kissed him because I think he needed me to kiss him. No, I kissed him because after these three weeks, I needed to—I needed to feel human, to feel...love. I needed to feel alive. I kissed

him not because he was Iraqi and I was American, or I
don't know—maybe because he was Iraqi and I was
American. I kissed him—because I had to do something.

Mouth to mouth, we breathe together, until at last…he
kisses me back, speaking his heart with his native tongue.
And for a moment, a very brief moment, everyone else
disappears. All the other stories vanish. The only story that
exists is the one we are writing, here together.

"Habibti," he says to me—my new favorite word. And
looking deeply into my eyes adds, "I am in the stars with
you."

"Nejoom," I say to him, remembering, smiling, before
I kiss him again, feeling blissfully nothing for the first time
in weeks.

At last. I can breathe.

*   *   *

Later, much later that night, far later than I should be in
Omar's apartment, lying in the crook of his arm where we
discover my head fits perfectly, I look up at him from his
heart, under his art. He is crying.

"Shukran, Kim," he says, "You saved me." I look deep
into his brown eyes. "I was dying before you find me." I
see a sea of both sadness and relief.

I want to say, "You saved me too, Omar. I was so lost I could no longer breathe—these stories, these weeks flattened me. I needed to feel human again, to feel love. You gave that to me. Thank you, Omar. You saved me!" But I can't say a word. My words don't matter. My story doesn't matter. All I can do is look at him, touch his cheek and snuggle closer against him as a tear falls in the crook.

Hours later, walking down a neighborhood street in his adopted home of Syria, Omar and I are sporadically holding hands. Both of us occasionally trying it on for size, as we walk down the hill we walked up a few hours earlier. We are in dire need of sustenance.

"Yella. Let's go. We get shawarma. You need your strength." Omar says. I laugh. He is funny—and right. We laugh again. We are practically running down the busy streets, holding hands, chanting "Shawarma, shawarma!" I feel like I'm in some movie—a 1950's movie, where they have the funny phone rings.

Even though it's late, the streets are crowded and shops are open. There is a refreshing buzz around us in this city. Isn't it the middle of the night? I don't even know. We are drunk with romance and beer, more romance than beer. And I am also apparently intoxicated with this city, with the sights and sounds and smells. I love it. I love it here!

Damascus is like a dream from another century. I feel like I have stepped into a place of magic. It doesn't even seem real. The old architecture stuns me. The streets that actually feel old under my feet comfort me. The bits of the beautiful old language I hear in conversations as we walk charm me. The smell of spices and jasmine seduce me. Everything seduces me. I look at Omar. He already seduced me. But one look and I am seduced again: Beautiful, delicious, life-saving Omar. I am someplace I have never been and I never want to leave.

Suddenly he releases my hand. "Wait here, Kim, one minute please." I watch him run into a shop and talk with a friend behind the counter. They chat a bit and then his friend slides something in his hand. Money. Oh my God, it's money. He just went and borrowed money from a friend to pay for the shawarma. Suddenly, it is like the brakes are slammed on. Everything crashes to a halt. I am reminded of where I am and who Omar is: a borderline destitute refugee in a somewhat hostile host country. I feel guilty for what he just did—and grateful—but more guilty. I mean I have money. I can buy us a shawarma. I planned to buy us a shawarma. Now I wonder if I should offer to pay or just let him. I don't want to offend him. There's the Arab pride thing and all.

"Everything okay?" I ask, as he returns to my side.

"No problem. Come! Shawarma!" We pick up speed down the busy Damascene street, trying to recreate the moment.

I start to say something but then let it go. It's only a few bucks. I look over at him. This is his life—indebted to his Syrian friend to feed his American girl shawarma.

I will always remember that night, as long as I live. Even now years later, that night is as clear as if it happened yesterday. In spite of the coffee grounds or yes, maybe even because of them, something unpredictable happened that night—in the crook of his arm, something that I couldn't walk away from. I'm honestly not sure if I saved him or he saved me. All I know is the crook felt right, the crook felt like home.

*   *   *

"I believe the first step in rebuilding our country is to learn English, study in the U.S. and then return and help rebuild Iraq," nineteen-year old Ali tells me on a bus to the ancient city Bosra, south of Damascus the next day. Bosra is an important stopover city for folks en route to Mecca. We are en route to lunch.

There are about twelve college-age Iraqi students and two adult American ex-pats on this bus. They are all involved in an organization here in Damascus that helps Iraqis whose college life was interrupted by the war, get into American schools. All these kids are waiting placement in an American college or university. Ali is my partner for the day—my 'bus buddy'.

As bus buddies, we're supposed to talk and get to know each other. He's sweet. I like him, but after being up all night with Omar last night, I am exhausted. I know, I know. It's my own damn fault. But now I can barely stay awake, let alone focus on this young man especially given the lulling of the bus motion. As I try desperately not to doze, my brain is only focusing on one thing: Omar, Omar, Omar. What a night!

Ali interrupts my thoughts again. Damn it, kid! Ok, fine. Fine! I will focus on *this* Iraqi.

"I'm sorry what did you say Ali?" I try to say in very slow English, although his is quite good. The bus makes a rather sharp turn and Ali leans into me.

"I say, we have no other choice. We need Americans to help us. It's the only way." He repeats.

Ali is right. His country needs help. We tore it down. We need to help build it up. Young people's education is only one part of it, but a crucial one. If children remain uneducated because of the war, aside from the moral issues that it presents, it sets up a huge national security problem down the line; an uneducated and angry Iraqi blaming his situation on America will pose many problems as he becomes very susceptible to extremists and their point of view. Clearly, if for no other reason, educating Iraqis serves a *security* benefit for the U.S. But of course, there are many other reasons. I meet a new reason every day.

But my brain can't handle all that right now. It's thinking about seeing Omar again for dinner tonight and what it will be like to look into those dreamy chocolate eyes again, after doing just that for the last seventeen hours. Against my better judgment, I am falling for him.

Ali is still talking. He's a good bus buddy. I am not. I refocus.

"Four years of my life have been wasted. I do nothing. This time is forever gone. But as long as I have a future, I don't care." Ali is a smart kid and isn't asking for much. After all, he left his family and home for the mere *possibility* of a future, not even a guarantee.

"My parents sent me all alone on a bus to Syria to stay here with this organization, even though placement in U.S. is not guaranteed and even though it was dangerous. This was my only chance. They say to them: Ali, he is your son now."

We finally pull up to the city walls of Bosra and I look up at the ancient ruins all around. Ali's parents gave up their son so he could have a chance at a new life, out of the ruins of Iraq.

*   *   *

I meet Omar in my hotel bar. He looks uncomfortable. I want to stay and relax and just have a drink. I try to smile and flirt with my vacation boyfriend. But he just sits there stiffly until eventually he asks if I mind if we just go up to my room. Forward, I think.

"More privacy," he says.

We order room service, eating mostly in silence, both of us maybe a bit nervous or uncertain, wondering how we got to here. I mean, we barely know each other.

We quietly discuss families, school and life in Iraq. He asks me almost begrudgingly about life in America. I don't feel like answering. Was I mistaken? Is our chemistry gone? Was this just a breath?

He stands, kisses me and says he should go home. "I think it not good if I stay here tonight Kim. You understand?"

I sort of do, but not really. I want him to stay. I think it would be fine for him to stay. He's already here after all! But I don't tell him anything. I just nod. Our worlds are so different. What do I know.

He kisses me again and says he would like to see me tomorrow. I nod again. Then Omar walks out. I stand for a bit at the door wondering what to do.

Oh crap. Omar.

*   *   *

My colleagues and I are at *The Center for Victims of Torture*. (You know you're going to have a good time there!) We are in your standard conference room, with the added bonus feature of torture posters and books everywhere and are sitting at a very large conference room table across from five people who have been tortured, most of them visibly so. It doesn't matter if it shows externally or not. You can always see it. How can we cause so much pain to fellow human beings?

I have to confess; I find myself *looking* for their scars, for their signs of torture and then feeling guilty once I see them — as if I am seeing their secret. They all have scars of course, inside and out.

We sit vaguely smiling at each other, waiting for the conversation to start, unsure how to begin. They are hesitant to answer our questions. We are hesitant to ask them.

Oh! I didn't even notice that one guy's missing fingers until just now. He is missing about half his fingers. How'd

I miss that? The man in the corner with one eye starts to talk.

"There is no place for us in Iraq now. No place called home. Iraq is ruined, now just a place for militia." He looks simply resigned. "You stole our life. You stole our laughter. You even stole parts of our bodies." You. America. He's right. We did do this, or at least we started it. We are culpable, like it or not.

I notice a huge scar from his left ear down his jaw to his chin. I hadn't seen that earlier. "This is big injustice done to the Iraqi people, you know. Let me tell you, I knew a man who had one leg tied to a tree and the other leg tied to the wheel of a car. The car, it just slowly went—forward, backward, forward, backward, forward, backward, until the man was…" he pauses, "…torn in two. That man was my friend. He was my friend. You understand?" We all say nothing. Do nothing. "There are things you can't imagine," he adds, crying.

And now I can't stop imagining it.

I look around the room, trying to stop imagining it, to get a different image. Anything.

The air in this room now feels heavy, weighted. I think about Omar. Wonder what he saw.

I want to get out of here. I don't like this place. I don't like these stories. All these victims must have come here to tell their stories and get help once upon a time. Now they are here telling *us* their story. I wonder if anybody is comfortable here. I'm not. Who's next with their horrific story? I shift in my seat.

A woman and a man suddenly emboldened by the last story both start to speak. They keep interrupting each other though, as neither will yield. They both want their turn to talk and they want it now. I don't know whom to look at. They are both demanding attention.

"Freedom? What freedom did you bring, America?" the man with missing teeth loudly asks me.

"My brother was killed! Killed by the militias. I have no one." The young woman with her feet blown apart by an IED desperately implores.

Perhaps as avoidance, I keep morbidly seeking scars. What else am I not seeing? What else am I missing? Where else are the scars?

A quiet man, the one absent-mindedly rubbing his missing fingers is looking at me. I look at him. He almost smiles.

I wait for the others to finish and then ask him through the translator, "Will you tell us your story?" He hesitates and continues to rub his finger stubs. He's handsome, I notice for the first time. In another lifetime, he would have women swooning all over him, including myself. Although maybe a little young for me, I will grant you, but cute nonetheless. I smile again. We are all only human, after all.

"I'm a poet. I write poems," he says through the translator. "Out of suffering, poets are born," he adds with a half-smile. He's got a sense of humor; his charm grows.

Would we like to hear a poem? Yes, yes, of course we would. I try to be subtle, but I can't stop looking at his missing fingers; and he can't stop fingering them.

"I always carry poems with me—here," he gestures to his pocket. "I carry them...because I can't...I...sorry. When I was kidnapped...my head. I...they...my memory no good, so..." He is gesturing to his head with his broken hand. I look at him—this tortured man with no memory who still writes poems.

"So..." he continues, "It's a love poem." We all pause at this announcement, caught off-guard. He must have noticed because he responds with, "Yes, you know I still believe in love!" As though to say 'What did we expect? How could he not?' We share of moment of embarrassment. We are all only human, after all.

"I am looking for love," he simply states, looking at the women in the room. Still a player. Then with his crinkled poem held in his broken fingers, he reads us one called "Turning Point" about missing body parts and being left by a woman, alone and broken.

The room is silent as he reads the last line, "Give me back my broken and dispersed parts, my love, so that I may live."

I am overwhelmed. There are so many broken and dispersed parts in this room. We are all only human, after all. We are all of us looking for love.

*   *   *

Omar and I are walking hand in hand in the souk of the old city of Damascus—and it is an old city. Looks it. Feels it. Smells it. Shops and shishas and shh… I am transported — oh my Omar. I roll around in this moment for a while, eager to make it last forever. I look around. Rows of spices line the walkway and then rows of hookahs and then rows of tapestries. It never ends. It's a miracle. I love markets. Shopping the souk with a sexy Iraqi man in Damascus? Priceless.

We met on a pre-designated street corner this morning. He called out my name. Kissed my cheek discreetly and everything felt good again. Last night feels like a dream. It must have been my overactive imagination last night. *This* is my Omar.

We just finished looking at the ultra famous Umayyad Mosque. Gorgeous. I brought a cute scarf to wear on my head in the mosque but was apparently still showing too much legs/boobs in my shapely dress, and so the security/morality police had me put on a full-length, gray polyester robe and matching hijab. I looked about as far from sexy as you could imagine I wanted to look on my daytime date with Omar. Laughing, he insisted on taking my picture while wearing this getup. I'm sure I fooled everyone as to my tourist/religious status.

Out of the mosque now and thankfully de-robed, hair blowing in the wind, we walk boldly hand in hand. Puritans be damned (or in this case…Islamic fundamentalists).

People are looking at us, or maybe they're not. It's hard to tell, and I could care less. I am over the moon in love with this man. Omar *is* the man in the coffee grounds. He is my destiny.

Several Syrian men approach. Omar quickly drops my hand. I look at him, trying to act casual, sensing his fear. The men pass. Then after a safe distance, he picks it up again and acts as though nothing just happened. Wait. What just happened?

Reading my mind, he responds, "They would not like it." Ah right, I think: unmarried man and woman holding hands, Middle East, not good. We're not in America anymore, Toto. I had almost forgotten.

But not finished, he continues, "It is not just because we are unmarried. It is also because you are American and I am Iraqi. Could be problem."

Really? Because I'm from America and he's from Iraq? This is his life. I drop *his* hand this time. I don't want to cause him trouble.

We walk a bit more, silently, not holding hands, each of us lost in our own separate thoughts, when I hear the call to prayer in the distance. Ah! I take a few steps towards the direction of the sacred music and stop.

This is one of my favorite parts of this part of this part of the world—the call to pray. I love the call to prayer. We don't have anything like this as Lutherans. I mean, come on. The closest thing we get to a haunting melody beckoning us to pray is Garrison Keillor's theme song. I'm jealous. I mean, don't get me wrong, I don't want to have to stop to pray five times a day by clockwork, but I definitely appreciate a good send up to God and there is something very old-world-charming about this tradition. Something comforting about it.

We listen to the enchanting music a moment longer. Omar stands behind me a bit. I am hypnotized. It's so melancholy, or maybe that's just me. I look at Omar, as hypnotized by him as I am by the music. We smile and gently he takes my hand once again.

Haram is as Haram does. Or whatever the Arabic equivalent is.

*   *   *

"I am like everyone else, Kim. I want to live somewhere safe. This is what I dream of, Kim. I want to have a chance at life like everyone else does," Omar tells me late that day, sitting in a café on some side street outside the city walls. I nod. I understand. Everyone deserves that. I *want* Omar to have that. I want all Iraqis to have that—a chance.

At his suggestion, we are drinking Turkish coffee. There is a God. I do so heart Turkish coffee.

By the time the far-too-small coffee is almost gone and I'm pondering the value of a second cup, Omar and I discover we are exactly the same: we both want kids, we both are very close to our families, we both love to laugh, we both have been single a long time, we both believe in God but detest what people do in the name of religion, we both love beer aaaaand we both think I'm beautiful. Okay, maybe that last one was just him. We each take a final glorious sip before the dregs and smile at each other. There's something here. God help me, there is something here. I feel like I have known him forever and I tell him so.

"I feel that too, Kim," he says, "It is so easy to talk to you. I feel I love you."

I tell him to shut it, to stop saying such crazy things, but inside I feel the same. I have fallen for this Iraqi refugee living in Syria. Holy. Crap. I have fallen for Omar.

Are we really as different as we are led to believe? Because honestly, we kinda seem the same—it's just he's Iraqi and I'm American. Big woop.

```
=======================================
```
KIM'S ARABIC DICTIONARY final installment:
Cipro The anti-diarrheal medication I really should
            have brought on this trip. I mean, really
            should have brought.
```
=======================================
```

We are walking in yet another charming part of Damascus. I just bought a charming orange embroidered shirt in another charming souk. It's all charming. It's all old. It's all romantic. But I can hardly be bothered with it anymore because — TMI — I have explosive, uncontrollable diarrhea. Yes. That's right, you heard me. I'm sorry, but I have diarrhea in the worst degree. Thank you Syria! Why did I bring no Cipro? Why!

Throughout this second day of walking and romancing, exploring the streets and galleries, I have been ducking into every bathroom I can find out of vile necessity. But I am still in denial. I refuse to be sick on this day. It's my day off and Omar and I are spending it together. I refuse to let this happen *now*. I've been in the Middle East for a month and felt fine. Today is NOT the day I get sick from the water or the food or the *whatever* here. It is NOT!

Yes. Yes, it is. After forcing myself to try to eat with Omar at this lovely local restaurant he chose, and with Omar ordering all the traditional dishes for me to sample and insisting on paying even though I know he has no money, I am sitting in the bathroom stall after having made my second quick exit, now making every bargain I can with God. No dice. All is not well in my bowels. Omar is going to suspect something. The jig is up. I could only force down a bite or two at lunch, or risk throwing up as well and I've been in here too long. He'll be on to me. Damn it diarrhea—not romantic!

"I'm so sorry," I say, in the restaurant doorway, returning after my second trip to the bathroom. His face is showing concern. "Do you mind if we cut this short? I'm not feeling well."

"Yes, I thought so," Omar responds, onto my ruse.

Twenty minutes later, we are somehow lying side by side on my hotel bed, arms and legs entwined, me running to the toilet every few minutes, as Omar laughs and laughs. Lord help me, I think, this must be love.

*　　*　　*

I am holding Omar's hand as he whistles while we walk. He is happy. I smile.

The sun is setting on our last day together in Damascus. It has been a lovely afternoon, despite my now only-mildly-screaming bowels. I could listen to him whistle forever. Stupid love. I squeeze his hand. We are both happy. We pass a flowering bush. He stops.

"Do you know this plant?" he asks. Um, no. Generally speaking, I don't know plants. A botanist, I am not.

"This is...how you say...yanni...jasmine? Yes, jasmine. Very famous in Iraq. I grow up smelling this. Jasmine all over Baghdad. Every time I smell it, I am reminded of home, of Iraq. I hope I can go back home someday," he adds sadly.

I take a whiff. It's strong. I recognize the smell, of course. It reminds me of department store perfume samplers. I look at him. He is lost for a moment in his memories—memories of his homeland. I try to imagine what it might be like in Baghdad with Omar when he shows me his jasmine, when we walk along the streets of his childhood, in the country of his past—someday, when it is safe in Iraq for an American and an Iraqi to smell flowers together. Maybe Omar is thinking the same thing. Or maybe he's afraid he will never return and the jasmine will be gone, all blown to smithereens.

"Yella," Omar says abruptly. And off we go, with him whistling a different tune, having completely forgotten the first.

*　　*　　*

Do you know I never asked Omar his "refugee" story? Isn't that incredible? I never asked him why he left, what happened, who died. I spent three weeks asking every Iraqi I met to tell me their story: What do you remember? What's your story? Tell me about all the horrors that have happened to you!

But by the time I met Omar, I guess I was just—full. I was so full. So somehow, I never asked his story.

How could I have never asked Omar his story?

The stories are sometimes all they have left.

Oh my God. Fakher. I have completely forgotten about Fakher. I didn't tell you about Fakher. Fakher's story changed me; it changed everything. I know you may not want to, I mean love is more fun than death right? But I need you to listen — to listen to one more story.

*　　*　　*

We were in Amman, Jordan and I had to pee. I really had to pee. Too much tea. If I didn't find a toilet soon, it was all over.

We were being shepherded down to the basement of this building to meet with this black Iraqi man and his family. Very exciting! Diversity! Black Iraqi! But first things first, I had to pee.

"Please sit," the agency host offered, gesturing towards a hard chair, with nary a toilet in sight.

"Oh thank you, shukran! But first I must…"

"Asalaam Al-Ayakoum," reverberated from the corner. A tall, handsome, black Iraqi man had risen and offered his hand with the greeting. Crap. The refugee I was supposed to meet was already there. Fakher is his name, I was told.

Crapity crap. I thought I still had a minute.

"Asalaam Al-Ayakoum," I returned begrudgingly, caught now in the interview.

More pleasantries were exchanged and I made a decision to try to hurry through the interview, as my bladder was beckoning. I sat down and started to ask questions from our little questionnaire sheet. But he kept interrupting me. Or maybe I kept interrupting him. Hard to say, my mind was not completely present.

"First, we thank God for everything," he started.

"I'm sorry, can you tell us your name and age?"

Somewhat awkwardly he did and then began again. Still not picking up on the cues that he wanted to do this his way, I interrupted again.

"Are you originally from Baghdad?"

"No," he politely answered, "South of Baghdad."

We volleyed like this a few more times, my bladder totally howling, drowning out my usually better listening skills. I should have just excused myself is what I should have done, but I didn't want to be rude. So instead I was rude.

Finally, he said, "Please. Let me tell you my story. I need to tell you my story. My way."

Okay, I finally listened. Full bladder and future UTI be damned: I was listening.

"We were looking forward to a future in America. But we recently found out, we were rejected," he said. "I wish to ask again, Insha'Allah because I made mistakes in interviews. I used to suffer from...mental difficulties, because of...what happened. It all returned to me during interview. This is why I was rejected, of course."

He was sad. Stoic, but sad. I could see it in his eyes. He had seen too much.

"As black Iraqi, it is difficult here in Jordan. We are not accepted. It is hard enough being Iraqi, worse being black Iraqi. Sara and Saif get made fun of in school, called Sudanian. My boys cannot even go to school."

I wanted to ask why specifically, but was afraid of being scolded again. So I waited, and sure enough, eventually the answer came.

"They must work. I watched my youngest son collecting cans on the road to sell yesterday. I did not like it. I had asked him to do this, of course, but I did not like it. I went up to him and said, 'Someday son, I hope you do not have to do this.'"

He paused.

"I will not tell my story in front of the children. They will have to leave. "Baba en tu et la-ru bara," he said to them in the language they all understood. First time anyone had ever had their children leave the room. They always tell their story in front of the children. "Why not?" they would ask and then usually add, "They lived it too." The children didn't want to leave. Apparently it's fun here. I did! I wanted to leave! Check please! But I stayed put. I could tell I was going nowhere for a while. I willed my bladder back into submission. When we were finally alone, he continued softly.

"One day, last week, I find a long stick in our room, a metal stick. This is strange. So I go to my eldest son, Mouhassein—he is fourteen and ask about this stick. He says, 'I planned to use it as defense against some of the meaner children, to protect myself, father.' I tell him…I tell him not to defend himself, to just take it, that we cannot risk being thrown out of this country for such trouble. You can imagine, of course, how hard this is for me to tell my son. But this is our life. I can change nothing."

My bladder no longer seemed important. We all took a breath.

He continued, "I used to be a hero. In Iraq, I was part of a famous artist family—very famous—singer, writer, dancer, playwright, even hairstylist! I was famous painter—very well known. We were very happy. But things did not stay this way, of course. This is what happens with war.

"Iraq became much more religious after fall of Saddam. My neighbor is Sunni and I am Shia, but before this, we do not care or even know what the other is. What does it matter? But then lines were drawn and everyone makes a group amongst themselves and you have no choice but to choose. You are either for me or against me.

"In the beginning, my family got threatening letters, bullets left in mailbox, gunshot fired in home. But you never knew who your enemy was. Is it your neighbor or is he still your friend?

"One day, I am in my yard when two strangers walk to my neighbor's house, push inside, and drag my neighbor out. I do not know what to do. So I hide and do nothing. The wife of course, panics, does everything she can but no one knows anything. And after three days, they find his broken body nearby." He looked at me. "This is only part of my story." I nodded, afraid of the rest.

Fakher was now sitting upright, straight as a rod and yet so frail. I could have pushed him over with a leaf. When his neighbor was taken, he did nothing. Nothing. I could see the weight of that choice on his shoulders and embedded in his heart. He needed to tell his story; that much was clear. I'm not even sure I needed to be here for it. But here I was.

"One day…one day, I open my front door and see a head—a human head on my fencepost." I just looked at him. "Do you hear me? A decapitated head." Fakher cried out. That last bit stopped by heart a bit. My jaw inadvertently dropped and I inhaled sharply.

"I quickly push my children back inside the house and close the door. They are crying, of course, frightened. They saw. There is a note on the head attached to an earring. But I cannot tell you what it says. I cannot read the note…too much blood."

I started to speak.

"Please," he interrupted. "I need to finish."

"I did everything I could to shield my wife and children," he pleaded, "You must know. But they see and hear, of course. How can they not? On more than one day we find bodies in our yard. Just thrown. Decapitated bodies. In our yard." His eyes were full of tears while mine were running down my face. I no longer cared.

"I try to ask questions, to find out why? Who? But people become suspicious. Then one day, I am taken—my turn. But I do not know by whom. What militia are they? Because I do not know this, I do not know what I should tell them. Should I tell them I am Sunni or Shia or...who do they think I am?" he yells. He was almost desperate at this point. I wanted to touch him, something.

"So I tell them I am Sudanian," he laughed. " 'Ana Sudani!' I said to them. For one whole day, they torture me and beat me, 'Ana Sudani!' They pull out my fingernails; ask me ridiculous questions over and over. 'Ana Sudani' is all I say, 'Ana Sudani! Ana Sudani!' "

He stopped, at last. I wasn't sure either of us was breathing. There was only dead silence.

"At last, they let me go. They kick me out of a car at the end of a road. After I fall out of the car, I stay still— certain they will shoot me in the back. But I do not know what else to do. So I just get up and...walk. At this moment, I forget everything—my religion, my family, my faith, everything." At that point, he was crying. This tall hero of a man had tears pouring down his face.

And yet the story continued, long past the point any of us wanted it to. I didn't want to hear anymore. I couldn't hear anymore. I wanted to pee. I wanted to scream. "HE IS A HUMAN BEING! LOOK WHAT WE LET HAPPEN TO A HUMAN BEING!" But like him, I sat still and said nothing, listening to this "collateral damage" tell his story.

"Please. I must tell you. There's more." No more.

"That day, I send my family away to live with my in-laws in Kabul and I flee to South of Iraq, where I am told it is better for Shia. I get a job as blacksmith, making…metal beams, metal sticks." He half-laughed, perhaps remembering the stick his son had wanted to use for defense. Irony was clearly not lost on this man.

"None of us trust each other there, always looking with suspicion, worried the other will kill us, ready to defend ourselves with our metal sticks! But I need this job—I am eating food humans should not eat. Then finally, one day, I wake up alone to find my little house on fire."

Please God, make this story stop, I remember thinking.

"Somebody is trying to kill me here too, of course. I know not who. I try to put out flames. I think, of course, someone will come and help. No one does. No one. The flame and smoke get worse. But I do not leave. The roof starts to fall on me, but I do not leave. I think to myself if no one comes to help or no neighbor calls my name to come outside, I will not leave. I will die in here.

"At this point, I cannot breathe. I start to panic and cry and scream, certain I will die: 'Is this what you want? Is it?'

"Finally I hear neighbors calling my name and doing what neighbors should do. They put out fire and save me.

"That day, I borrow money and go to Kabul, to my wife and children. My in-laws want us to leave Iraq, of course. But I am scared. I know I will never come back if I leave my beloved country… But one look in my children's eyes and..." At last he paused.

"This is my story."

We said nothing for a very long time. I looked at him. He looked at me. He breathed. I breathed, as that seemed like all we were able to do. He dropped his eyes down. I followed suit.

"What do you feel?" I finally inadequately offered.

"It's hard to say what I feel—mostly nothing." He was still not looking at me. "Sometimes, sometimes I feel like a bat. I only come to life at night. Maybe I am crazy. I don't know. Sometimes at night, when I drink, though, I get in the mood to paint. I want to express myself, but I can't. I don't know how to anymore…it is very difficult to forgive. I used to be a hero."

Once our interview was over and I was finally sitting in the bathroom stall, I couldn't stop crying. I just sat on the toilet and sobbed. I cried for all he lost. I cried because he had to tell this story at all. I cried because it was so important to him that he did. I cried because in his eyes, he is no longer a hero. I peed and I cried. I cried and I peed.

But that's not the end of the story. It's never the end.

As we said our shukrans and goodbyes, Fakher looked me squarely in the eyes and in Arabic said, "Do not cherry-pick my story. Do not just tell pieces. Tell it all. Tell my *whole* story so that the world may know."

Nothing is in order anymore. Endings. Beginnings. Past. Present. I can't remember. I don't want to remember. It's all a blur. I can't take any more stories.

There was another interview, in Lebanon maybe? I'm not sure. What I do remember is feeling it's so loud in here. Everyone is trying to get their story heard! I can't understand anybody and yet they're all vying for my attention. My head hurts. I'm tired. I need lunch.

"Uncle killed in Iraq...Al Qaida," one brother announces in broken English. Another brother responds in Arabic, and then the wife speaks saying something, but even the translator can't keep up. They're talking too fast and all at once.

"We cannot live like this," someone else shouts in Arabic.

"Our brother who was killed worked for U.S. Forces. You want to see his paperwork? Here, I show you." Mom is talking, Dad is talking, kids are talking, too.

There are about twelve family members here, all living in this small apartment and in another just down the street. Every one of them has a story to tell: "We all live here...such small apartment...our children...some days we don't eat so the children can...we sit all day...nothing to do...America! Please..." I'm trying to look at who is talking, but it is pure chaos in here. It's almost white noise. And in that white noise, I realize I am thirsty. I am so thirsty.

I lift my fancy teacup from the little plastic table in front of me. This is a beautiful china tea set they are serving us from. It must have come from Baghdad. Most of the Iraqi's nice possessions came with them from Baghdad. There is no money for such things now.

People are still almost shouting. I wonder if this is what family dinners are like. I sip my tea, lost in it all. Everything. Some members of this family are angry, some are just insistent, but all are talking—loudly.

One of my colleagues at last gets in a question, inquiring about any Iraqi music or stories or dances they can share with us, and for the first time, the room goes silent. No one has anything to say. No one can offer up any song or poem or story for us. Nothing.

"We have no memory for that anymore."

"Please. Say nothing, Kim," Omar is holding my face between his palms looking deep into my eyes. It's our last night before I leave Syria and I'm not ready for this to end.

"But Omar, I leave tomorrow! Don't you want to spend tonight with me? I just have this closing final dinner thingy. It'll only be a few hours. You can stay here in my hotel room. Or you can come back later! Just come back later!" I try to convince him, pulling him towards the chair.

"No, I should go now. It's better we say goodbye now, I think."

"But I don't want to say goodbye," I counter. Do not cry, Kim. Do not cry. He faces me and we look into each other's eyes. Fail. He rubs his thumb along my cheekbone, wiping a big, juicy tear as it falls.

"Habibti…" he tries to soothe me.

"Omar, I…"

"Shh…say nothing, habibti. There is nothing to say."

How can he say that? There is so much to say. I want to say how this has been the most amazing three days of my life; yes, I know it's only been three days but I think we have something here, that I want to come back and visit him again or I want him to come to me. I want to say that I have fallen in love with him and that I no longer want to live without him, that I can't live without him. But he won't let me say any of that. He is also crying now. Then he simply kisses me one last time and walks out of my hotel room, leaving me all alone.

The crowded room feels the impact of that. Then after a silent split second, two of the brothers talk back and forth in Arabic, almost teasing each other. Something is happening. I keep indicating by gesture and raised eyebrows to the translator to translate, but she seems enraptured with the conversation. She is smiling. What are they saying? Come on, translator! Translate!

The father joins in. They are all laughing now. What, what? The mother gestures for her son to start, and one of the adult sons starts to sing a song. The room implodes with laughter. They clap and cajole him until the other brother stands up, grabs the singing brother pulling him to his feet and joins him in song. I smile at what is beginning to happen. I no longer need the interpreter. It's perfectly clear what's happening: they are remembering.

The young children laugh the most at this rare happy spectacle in their makeshift home. The father stands up and starts a dance step and before you know it, the whole family is up singing and dancing.

Singing and dancing! *Their memories were returning.*

There is pure joy and abandon in this moment. It's beautiful. Everyone seems so happy. I soak it all in and am enjoying the show, until the mother comes to me and grabs my arm to join.

"No, no. La! La!" I offer fruitlessly. I just want to watch, to bathe in this happy moment. But she won't give up. So finally upon her insistence, realizing the importance of this moment for them, for us all, I relent, "Na'am, na'am. Yes." I laugh, abandon my modesty and join in the grand dance now happening in their small living room.

I look around at my dance partners and everything moves into slow motion, no longer in real time. We are in a circle—stepping and kicking, holding hands and laughing. The Dabke. They are trying to teach me the Iraqi dance. I see faces and smiles. I hear laughter and squeals.

The joy around me is palpable. Even amidst the chaos, I know this is an important moment, something I will always remember—the blissful, euphoric triumph of happiness and laughter over trauma and heartache, through music and art and yes, memory. We all are sharing it. I am a part of it and I am so grateful. These Iraqis, whose country was invaded and whose lives were devastated largely in part by my country, are letting us invaders and devastators share in this blissful moment with them. I revel in it. I swim in it. I dance and laugh and try to sing along in cobbled, mimicked Arabic, oblivious to anything or anyone else. Pure, unadulterated joy.

Until there is a crash. The room stops.

It's me. I think I may have just kicked over the table with the tea set. I look down. Shit. I did.

Shit. Shit. Shit.

This was probably their last prized possession, and I broke it. Shit, shit, shit. I am almost crying as I bend over to see if anything can be salvaged among the ruins, when the mother grabs my arm once again to stand me up.

"No," she emphatically declares looking me in the eyes, "Dance!"

"But…"

"Dance!" And the celebration continues as if nothing happened.

I want to pick up the pieces, to apologize, something, anything, but she is insisting with eyes of defiance, God bless her. She refuses to let this moment end—not yet anyway.

"Dance!" she orders.

I stand there in my hotel room for a few moments, not knowing what to do, silently sobbing—for Omar, for me, for everyone, for all of this. I open the door to my hotel balcony and step outside, this time front and back sobbing. After a moment, I regain control. I'm better at that now, better at stopping the tears. The evening air is cool. I breathe deep, trying to figure out what just happened, if this was love or just...CPR.

The cool breeze blows against my tears, drying them. Did my coffee ground lady get Omar and my Bedouin camel man confused? Did I? Did I already get my marriage proposal? Should I just walk away?

I watch Omar walk away, crossing the street from the hotel heading home. He pauses at the far corner of the intersection and looks back at me. We share something resembling a moment. I half smile.

What do I do?

"Dance!"

And so I do. We all do. We dance for all those who can't. We dance for all that has been lost. We dance for the possibility of a new beginning. We dance for the possibility of an end. We dance. Amongst the shattered shards and ruined treasure, we all dance and laugh and sing and holler until we can't anymore—a few moments of fleeting, crackling, broken joy.

Three Days in Damascus

Three Year Intercontinental Internet Relationship

I am half dead. Lying on the couch on my apartment in New York, I can't stop thinking of Omar and replaying each story all the refugees told me. I am on a continuous loop, a non-stop, never-ending, 24/7, all-Iraqi-all-the-time loop.

I have been back home three days now, but haven't moved much from this spot on my couch thanks to the loop. I feel exhausted, disoriented, and actually shell-shocked. I have never felt like this before and don't know what to do. My thoughts and actions don't seem to be my own. I don't feel like myself. I feel paralyzed, unable to do anything. All I can manage is to feed my cats and myself a bit and then lay back down.

Earlier today I noticed a pen that has been lying on the floor since I returned home. I bent over and picked it up. That seemed like enough for one day.

*　　*　　*

"You're in love with an Iraqi man? Oh my God! How did this happen?" my best friend Catherine bellows at my neighborhood pub in New York, over the most amazing bacon cheeseburgers I may have ever eaten. God, I missed bacon. I am so happy *not* to be eating hummus right now and truth-be-told, happy to be off my couch.

"Oh my God!" my other best friend Randy agrees, as I chew more amazing meat, home at last.

But "Omayyad!" is all I hear. Omayyad. The Omayyad Hotel was the last place I saw Omar. *Standing in my hotel room, crying, I didn't know what to say. So I said nothing, wrapped in his arms.* The whole thing is like a dream now. It's all a dream. All the Iraqis I met. All the stories. All the kidnappings and killings, all the horror and heartbreak, all the torture and terror, all the shukrans and shawarmas. It feels like a dream. But it's real. They're all real. And sadly, Omar and all the Iraqis are probably in the exact spot I left them—waiting.

I stop eating with that realization. Full stop.

"Kim," Catherine's voice across the table from me pulls me back to the restaurant. "Tell us."

I want to tell them where my thoughts all just went: to all the Iraqis I met and stories I heard, to how much work we have to do as a nation to set this right, to how empty and annihilated I feel, but it's too much. I can't. I can't start yet. I need some time. Besides, Catherine and Randy didn't really want any of that now. They want the steamy gossip, the juicy juice, the unexpected events that led to their best friend returning stateside with an Iraqi refugee boyfriend in virtual tow, when all she was supposed to do was interview him.

I snap out of it and I take another bite of my exquisite cow and pig. "I have no idea how it happened," I say. "How does anything happen?"

My brain travels back again. And I realize the Iraqis are all probably asking the same thing: "How did this happen?" while sitting in their plastic patio chairs, in their temporary homes, waiting for change—or something.

*　　*　　*

I just hung up the phone with Omar.

I talked to Omar today! Only for like three minutes, but I talked to Omar today! He messaged me about twenty minutes ago. For the first time. A message. On Yahoo. From Syria. From Omar. He messaged me! So I called him. Just a regular phone call. I don't have any idea how much it will cost and honestly I don't care. He did. He kept saying we should hang up, that it was too expensive. But I didn't care. I heard his voice. We laughed almost the whole time.

I can't believe I talked to Omar.

Three Days in Damascus

OMY. I have to see him again.

*   *   *

Email

Kim <schk@gmail.com>

To: <Omar_artist@yahoo.com>

Date: Wed, Oct 21, 2009 at 5:31pm

Subject: Good talk!

Hi,

OK, listen Omar. I don't know what to do about you. I miss you terribly. And it is ridiculous that we should even think about attempting a relationship together. But I am thinking about it. And I don't really even know how to do it. I guess through chat and email and I can call you. I miss you. And I think I do love you. I wish I were there or you were here now.

Please tell me more. Tell me more about what you were thinking about us. Tell me why you left me that last night. Tell me if you think this is real or just a fantasy on both of our parts. I need to know.

Flights are expensive, but I think if we keep talking and steadily writing each other and still like what we see of each other, maybe I will try to come back out to Damascus in November or December. And maybe you study English and I, Arabic...and maybe we can communicate better.

Three Year Intercontinental Internet Relationship

Omar...I just don't know if you're real or just a really, really great man I met on a trip I took.

OK, so when you can talk and are going to the internet cafe, you text me and I'll be online, ok? And if you say Yahoo is better then Skype is Syria, lets keep using yahoo. That's totally fine.

It was really good to hear your voice. You seemed close again. I wish you were...
k

*　*　*

I just laughed. Hard.

I am in my improv class. I teach improvisation, by the way, and this is my first class since I got back and I just laughed. A student said something funny and I laughed, instinctually. It felt nice, but now I feel bad, guilty. I don't want to laugh. It seems unfair somehow. Because, you know, refugees.

The improv scene continues, but I am barely there. I am thinking about Omar...and Fakher and Daoud and Saleema and the kids who wanted me to take them to America. I wonder where they are right now. I wonder if they're laughing. I wonder if they'll ever laugh again.

*　*　*

IM Nov 7, 2009

11:08:03 AM k: Omar!!!! ☺ Hi!! I miss you Omar! So much! Are you there?

11:10:39 AM k: Omar?

11:10:58 AM o: hello habebty I miss you too I wish u here

11:11:04 AM k: Can u talk now?

11:11:10 AM o: I sorry kim internet so bad maybe tomorrow

11:11:04 AM k: ☹

*   *   *

New York traffic bellows outside my fourth floor window of my apartment, as I eat my non-shawarma sandwich. I miss shawarma. I know I could go down to the East Village and get an almost authentic one, but that takes energy, which I still don't have much of these days.

So instead, I sit at my computer, by my cell phone, willing it to buzz with a text so I know Omar is online. I'm waiting. Always waiting.

Come on, Omar! Text me! This system we have in place where he texts me to tell me he is going to the internet café so that we can talk online is a pretty good system— except when he's late or forgets or gets otherwise distracted. If only he had internet in his home, we could talk whenever! First-world expectations. First-world delusions.

My attempts to integrate back into life here in the U.S. have not been easy. I am different and everything here feels the same. Omar is still my lifeline, it seems. When I talk to him, I feel okay again. I *need* my communications with him. It keeps me connected. But I just find his frequent disappearances disheartening. I try to understand—I mean, he is a refugee after all, living in Syria. Internet isn't always easy to find. It costs money. Blah, blah, blah. But it's hard. I feel like I'm not a priority and I want to be. Breathe Kim. His life sucks. You have freedom. Be patient.

I go back to my computer and try to focus. I need to write this damn play about my time in the Middle East and all I want to do is write about Omar. The non-profit organization that brought me there is waiting for the play. They want to know I'm making progress, which I'm not. I'm stuck, totally stuck when suddenly it dawns on me: What if the play is *about* Omar? Wait. I might have something here. Do I dare write a very personal play about falling in love with Omar? Is that what this play should be about?

The light bulb clicks and a car honks. I jump, automatically looking at my phone. Nope, that was not my phone. That was a car. Pull it together, Kim. No Omar today. Write your play. I sigh and wonder if it's worth it— a long-distance relationship with a refugee? Who does this?

*   *   *

IM Nov 8, 2009

11:15:29 AM k: Glad we could talk finally on the phone today Omar.

11:15:32 AM k: I like hearing your voice, makes me feel closer to you

11:15:39 AM o: me too kimmy

11:15:42 AM k: I am going to go for a bike ride today!

11:15:43 AM o: ok

11:15:58 AM k: do you know bike ride?

11:16:05 AM o: no

11:16:10 AM k: riding a bicycle

11:16:16 AM o: what it is?

11:16:20 AM o: wate I look dictsonary

11:16:26 AM k: Yay! Your dictionary is back!

11:16:28 AM k: 2 wheels

11:16:33 AM o: ahh yes

11:16:37 AM k: there's your english lesson for today!

11:16:45 AM o: thanks techar

11:16:49 AM o: u can do it?

11:16:53 AM k: ride bike? of course! Can't you??

11:16:59 AM o: yes of cors

11:17:10 AM k: Of course ☺ he says!

11:17:15 AM k: well then! why are you surprised I can?

11:17:31 AM o: becose

11:17:43 AM o: u dont till me that before

`11:18:03 AM k:` there's a lot I dont tell you ☺

`11:18:11 AM k:` we have a lot to learn.

`11:18:16 AM o:` and i think girls dont like it

`11:18:23 AM k:` really!

`11:18:30 AM k:` huh

`11:18:45 AM k:` maybe it's an american thing for girls

`11:18:49 AM o:` yes

`11:19:04 AM k:` Well, I like it

`11:19:06 AM o:` good let's do it together someday

IM Nov 9, 2009

`09:56:26 AM o:` Kim what you do now?

`09:56:35 AM k:` I'm trying to write my play

`09:56:47 AM o:` yes? oh god this is god

`09:56:52 AM k:` yes, very good ☺ and some of it is about you Ive decided!

`09:57:06 AM o:` relly kim?

`09:57:12 AM k:` really omar. ☺

`09:57:26 AM o:` kim i wont kiss you

`09:57:42 AM k:` won't or want? ☺

`09:57:52 AM o:` I sorry I not understand

`09:57:58 AM k:` It's ok. I joke. I want you to kiss me too. Invite me to your cam again

`09:58:02 AM k:` argh. It's not working. I want to see you!

`09:58:08 AM k:` says unavailable

`09:58:25 AM o:` way

09:58:30 AM k: dont know why

09:58:33 AM o: kim

09:58:43 AM k: yes, darling omar

09:58:54 AM o: you are butefol I love you

09:59:03 AM k: thank you

09:59:06 AM k: shukran ☺ I crazily love you too

09:59:18 AM o: you see me?

09:59:26 AM k: no

09:59:32 AM k: but we'll make it work....

09:59:41 AM k: tell me how you are

09:59:55 AM k: ahhhhhh wait camera might be working…

10:00:04 AM o: im good

10:00:13 AM o: and you

10:00:16 AM k: there you are! Yay

10:00:32 AM o: kim

10:00:38 AM k: omar

10:00:55 AM k: It's good to see you finally! Tell me about your
day yesterday…

10:01:25 AM k: oh no! pictures frozen again....

10:02:40 AM k: Argggg. life is so difficult for us!

10:02:48 AM o: beter than nothing

10:03:00 AM k: yup you're right

10:03:13 AM k: I'd rather have a frozen you than no you!

*   *   *

"Omar? Are you still there?" I type to him on instant messenger late one night. We had spoken earlier in the evening, but he wanted to instant message with his family. I have just been lying on my couch thinking and writing about him since then.

"Yes, habibti. I here," he answers a moment later. I'm so happy. I needed one more shot of him tonight.

"Why do you think we met that night, Omar?" I hesitate, then, "Do you understand the question I am asking?"

"Yes," he types. And then there is a pause, a long pause that makes me nervous. Does he understand? Does he not care? Is this as important to him as it seems to be becoming for me?

"It is something that shold be happen kim," he finally responds. I smile. What a lovely idea. It's something that should happen. He must have had to refer to his Arabic-English dictionary for some of those words. The thought of that charms me, the effort he made.

"I think you are a very special man, Omar," I say.

He is quiet again. I think he must be looking up the next heartful response he is going to say, when I realize: no, he's actually gone this time.

"Omar? Hello? Are you there?"

Nothing. The notification bar shows he's not connected anymore. Syrian internet must have gone out again.

Stupid internet. How am I supposed to build a relationship like this?

*   *   *

IM Nov 17, 2009

`10:11:22 AM k:` Omar so good to talk today. Talking is better.

`10:12:17 AM o:` Yes but cost more

`10:12:27 AM o:` Kim

`10:12:32 AM k:` Yes omar

`10:13:01 AM o:` i wont kiss you

`10:13:26 AM o:` i wont you here

`10:13:41 AM o:` on my arm

`10:13:49 AM o:` do u remember?

`10:13:57 AM k:` yes, I remember being on your arm. How could I forget?

`10:14:16 AM k:` Omar I miss you so much

`10:14:57 AM o:` me too kimy you so far away

IM Dec 1, 2009

`03:17:52 AM k:` Omar Where are you? We were supposed to talk at 3pm. Are you there?

`03:42:22 AM k:` Omar? I hate this. What's going on? Omar?

IM Dec 3, 2009

01:11:40 PM k: Omar I don't know where you went. I keep trying to call you.

01:47:44 PM k: Omar?

IM Dec 11, 2009

04:55:22 PM k: It's been over a week. I call you. You never answer. What's happening Omar?

*   *   *

A month later. Yes, a full month later, I finally heard from Omar.

At first, I spent the month sans Omar wondering if he was still alive, of course. I kept fearing he had been killed and that thought almost made me retch. Then I started worrying what I had done wrong. (Typical female response; makes me retch more.) How did I offend him so greatly as to have him walk away from what we both felt and declared as love? How do you walk away from that? Was I naïve? Did he just use me? All month, I replayed every conversation, I re-read every text, and I replayed every moment we spent together in Damascus. But nothing made sense.

So he must be dead. That was the only explanation that made sense! Omar is dead. Oh my God! Omar is dead??

That thought sent me into further oblivion until one day I get this text:

8:28:03 AM o: I love you. I am sorry for not being there and hearting you Kim. I hope we stay freands for ever you are a great wemon one day we should meeting agean. I want kiss you in your aes.

In my what, did he say? After a month of silence, this is what I get? I want to kiss you in your "ass"?

But I need more explanation than that, so I decide to call again and eventually he finally decides to pick up the phone.

"Omar." I am shocked.

"Hello, Kim." He replies sadly.

In the years to come, I will learn to know that sad voice, that sad Omar voice quite well. We will bring out each other's sad voices quite often unfortunately.

"You're alive."

"Yes, I am sorry, Kim." There is a long pause—me not knowing, him hesitating. "I don't know what say," he finally says.

Neither do I apparently, because we both say nothing. (Note: Silence on an international call is wasted money.)

"Where did you go, Omar?" I ask. My question is met with more silence.

"I am sorry, Kim. I..." And then he stops.

He what? *What?* He says nothing. We sit in silence, worlds apart.

He finally picked up my call and this is the conversation we are having. Kill me now.

"I am no good. Maybe you fell for the wrong Iraqi." These are the words I hear coming out of Omar's voice thousands of miles away from me.

"What did you say?" I ask, in tears from this torturous conversation. My kitty on my lap looks up at me with pity.

"Maybe you fell for the wrong Iraqi, Kim."

Neither of us says anything for a very long time. More silence. More wasted money. I have to find a better international rate plan.

"Well, you're the Iraqi I fell for, so that's that."

* * *

Tomorrow I leave New York flying to the Midwest to be with my family for Christmas. I haven't seen them since my life got turned upside down in Damascus. I am packing my already stuffed suitcase. I'm frustrated. I always pack too much. I try to squeeze in another shirt. It's the orange embroidered shirt I bought in the Damascus souk that day with Omar. I love this shirt and it gives me pause. I miss Omar. We have only sporadically messaged online since our last phone call. I am keeping my distance. "Maybe you fell for the wrong Iraqi" echoes in my head. Maybe I did. I feel sick by the thought of it.

I stand there for a moment at the edge of my bed thinking.

Why would he just disappear on me? We were in love. We said that. I thought we did. It just doesn't make sense. Was he running away? I don't get it. His behavior is erratic and…stupid. Does he have P.T.S.D.? Or is he just an A.S.S.?

No, no, no! With a heavy sigh and a shake of my head, I toss the stupid orange shirt on my chair and pull the zipper stubbornly around my bag without it. I need to move on, to forget about Omar. Omar is a dead end. Dead. End.

*　　*　　*

IM Dec 25, 2009

05:53:16 PM o: Mery chrismas kim

IM Jan 16, 2010

02:17:10 PM o: Kim I look for you online you are never here
02:17:27 PM o: Kimy?

IM Jan 19, 2010

04:33:42 PM o: I sorry. Please talk kim. I miss you.

And that night, he called me for the first time ever. And I picked up.

PHONE CALL RECAP: Romance. Forgiveness. Love. Romance. Forgiveness. Love.

* * *

And then the next day…

09:48:27 AM o: hi

09:51:17 AM k: hi

09:54:56 AM o: wow

09:55:09 AM k: wow?

09:55:44 AM o: cute u r cute is all

09:55:56 AM k: thank you

09:56:05 AM k: I'm glad u called yesterday. It was good to finally talk

09:56:29 AM o: I know. i wish im there kimmy

09:56:32 AM k: me too ☺

09:56:38 AM k: Will you not say anything else?

09:56:48 AM o: I miss you

09:56:56 AM k: Oh omar…

09:57:34 AM o: I know, Kim. It's so hard you know. You know my sitchwashion here

09:57:44 AM k: I know omar. You just confuse me so much. And you hurt me by disappearing

09:57:56 AM o: kim i want kiss you in your aes

09:57:42 AM k: In my what?

09:57:26 AM o: your aes

09:57:42 AM k: Oh! my eyes?

09:57:26 AM o: yes your aes

09:57:26 AM o: eyes

09:57:42 AM k: So funny. Last time you said that, I thought

09:57:26 AM o: what

09:57:42 AM k: Never mind ☺ I want you to kiss me too!

09:57:48 AM k: invite me to cam again

09:58:02 AM k: argh. It's not working

09:58:25 AM o: way

09:58:30 AM k: dont know why

09:58:33 AM o: kim

09:58:43 AM k: yes darling omar

09:58:54 AM o: you are butefol

09:59:03 AM k: thank you

09:59:06 AM k: shukran Omar ☺

IM Jan 29, 2010

09:40:10 AM k: you're online!

09:58:41 AM o: yes my love sorry. I talk with brother in baghdad

10:04:36 AM k: are they all ok?

10:04:52 AM o: can we talk in make

10:05:05 AM k: in make?

```
10:05:10 AM o: mace
10:05:28 AM k: I'm sorry I don't understand
10:05:30 AM k: oh mic! Microphone! OK ...
10:05:59 AM o: yes
10:06:43 AM o: kim my gad
10:07:30 AM o: you are so far
```

*　　*　　*

"Okay, Omar, habibi. I should go. I am so happy I got to talk to you on your birthday, but I need to take a nap before my rehearsal tonight."

We had just finished a romantic birthday phone call, all-dreamy and all-shary, all-birthday-y. I sighed, filled with all my Omar-lovey feelings.

"A nap?" he asks and then starts laughing loudly.

"What is so funny?" I am totally confused. "Omar?"

"A nap! What is this word, Kim? Nap? What is it?"

I start to laugh now.

"Kimy, what is nap? I must know!"

"A nap! It's like, um, a short sleep...in the day."

"Ah nap," he responds, still laughing. "I like this word: nap. I like it very much. I wish remember it."

"Oh, Omar. You make me laugh! Nap!"

"Nap! Nap, Kim. Ok, go take nap!" He is still laughing. "Nap!"

Three Days in Damascus

Sometimes I really like Omar.

*   *   *

IM Feb 25, 2010

02:14:18 PM o: yes what kim

02:14:38 PM k: I dont know if I should trust you...

02:14:44 PM o: yes

02:15:49 PM k: I guess I don't know how you feel about me
honestly any more

02:16:07 PM o: kim

02:16:07 PM k: if you think we are destined to friendship

02:18:03 PM o: i thing what is betwen us is more than freanship

02:18:15 PM k: what is it then?

02:18:50 PM k: you must be honest with me

02:19:03 PM o: what u think?

02:19:11 PM k: I dont know anymore.

02:19:17 PM k: I thought it was love for a long time.

02:21:40 PM o: u r lake arab girl

02:22:02 PM k: quit calling me a needy arab girl. ☺

02:22:05 PM o: u understand ☺

02:22:25 PM k: I need honesty omar.

02:22:36 PM o: i am kimy

02:25:54 PM k: I want you to always be honest with me is all.

02:26:42 PM o: ok I am kim im honest

02:27:19 PM k: Because I'm in love with you.

02:27:24 PM k: and I can't move past you.

IM Feb 29, 2010

`10:33:02 AM o:` kim i wont sleep with you agean

`10:25:59 AM k:` won't or want?

`10:33:02 AM o:` want

`10:25:59 AM k:` Phew. Me too

`10:33:11 AM o:` rely?

`10:33:25 AM o:` bad girl ;)

*　　*　　*

I am sitting on my couch, holding my laptop on my lap, as is designed, while Omar and I have been having a successful IM *with* video for the past hour or so: a miracle of all miracles! He says something to make me laugh. He often makes me laugh.

"I like your laph," he types. I smile and snuggle into the couch a bit more.

"You're so far away, Omar."

"No, you are," he responds. "I am here." I smile again and start to laugh.

"I like your lagh so much, Kim. Your lagh is good." I look at him via our internet connection, trying to see into his eyes, while my smile recedes. This is stupid. I don't know if I should trust him again. Am I a fool to? Perhaps sensing my hesitation, Omar softly replies, "Open your heair to me."

"I'm trying Omar. I really am. It's just hard to trust you again. You hurt me so much last time you just disappeared on me."

"Please Kim."

"Oh, Omar…"

"Show me your *haer*," again appears on my screen.

"I'm *trying* Omar. It's just hard to trust you with my heart. It's really hard."

"No, Kim. Show me your hear. Open your heair for me."

Suddenly I realize I'm an idiot—an absolute idiot. I always assume something deep and emotional, when often it's not.

"Hair!? You're saying hair?" I gesture to my head. "Good Lord, Omar," I type. "You mean my ponytail?"

"Yes, Kim. Take down your hair so I see." Omar always prefers my hair down, not up. I start to pull out the ponytail holder holding it all in place and start to laugh again. Unbelievable.

"I like your laph, Kim."

*   *   *

IM Mar 4, 2010

09:39:42 AM k: so what did you do today?

```
09:40:48 AM o: shoping becose you know my mum is here
09:41:02 AM k: Yes of course! so glad! did she cook for you?
09:41:05 AM o: yes she is
09:41:06 AM k: nice
09:41:11 AM k: what is she making?
09:41:43 AM o: iraqi rice with meet and soop
09:41:51 AM k: yum
09:42:19 AM o: come ingoy with us
09:42:25 AM k: I would love to!
09:42:35 AM o: habebti ☺
09:42:42 AM k: habibi
09:43:00 AM k: does she know of me omar?
09:43:17 AM o: yes
09:46:45 AM o: u r besy?
09:46:52 AM k: No, just drinking coffee …in my pajamas ☺
09:47:19 AM o: i want see u open a cam
09:49:48 AM o: my mum want see you too
09:49:57 AM o: and say hello
09:50:15 AM k: NO....
09:50:19 AM k: hang on!! I'm not ready to meet your mom
09:50:39 AM k: look at your cute mom!
09:51:08 AM k: I love her!!!
09:51:29 AM o: your cam is closd kim why?
09:52:07 AM k: Because I am in little pajamas and look too
               naked!!
09:52:14 AM o: oh
```

09:52:21 AM o: thats ok kimy

09:52:46 AM o: i want u lake that

09:52:53 AM k: ha ha!! Your mom doesn't!

09:53:52 AM k: I like seeing you with her. You're cute together.

09:57:51 AM o: she want see you

09:59:50 AM k: shes lovely Omar

09:59:53 AM o: and she lake your laph

10:00:04 AM k: she can't hear me!

10:00:07 AM k: ok give me a minite to change

10:02:04 AM k: Ok I opened my cam

10:02:17 AM o: why you cheng your clothe?

10:02:37 AM k: becuase I needed to be decent to meet your
mom!!!!!!

10:02:44 AM o: hhhhhhhhhh

10:02:37 AM k: Where's your mom? I don't see her

10:02:54 AM o: kim my mom go to take nap

IM Mar 9, 2010

01:38:06 PM k: Omar!! Whered you go? I go to the bathroom and
you disappear!

01:38:15 PM k: come baaaaaaaaaack

01:38:17 PM k: ah here you are! Where'd ya go on me? ☺

01:38:33 PM o: I here. Sorry. fanta. See?

01:38:17 PM k: ah yes fanta! We have that here too! Yum!

01:39:32 PM o: Kim, why do you love me?

01:39:54 PM k: Wooh

01:40:05 PM k: I don't know, Omar. Many reasons. You tell me - - why me? Why me that night we met?

01:40:09 PM k: do u understand?

01:40:13 PM o: yes

01:40:19 PM o: i dont know why but i believe that its not by chance

01:40:28 PM k: we were meant to meet you think?

01:40:36 PM o: it is something that shold hapen

01:40:47 PM o: that what i thing

01:40:57 PM k: I think that too.

IM Mar 14, 2010

03:10:13 PM k: Youre so particular! ☺

03:10:23 PM o: But I don't like the bags. I tell you this before

03:10:28 PM k: I know I know! Loose leaf! You like loose leaf!

03:10:29 PM o: Yes, how you say?

03:10:33 PM k: loose leaf. You like loose leaf tea

03:10:43 PM o: Yes I am very important man kim

03:10:52 PM o: When I come u.s. you must make me looseleef

03:10:59 PM k: Yes of course i will!

03:11:02 PM k: As you wish important man!

03:11:12 PM o: Good. very good kim ☺

IM Mar 27, 2010

09:23:11 AM k: Hi Sweetie... I just tried calling you on a new phone card. Cheap! No answer though. Find me. Miss you.

IM Mar 28, 2010

`11:05:33 AM k:` hey omar. I keep trying to call you but you don't answer. What's going on? Hope everything is ok.

*   *   *

"Well, Kim, he's a refugee! It's not supposed to be easy." I am sitting with Catherine at our favorite diner. "But you must admit it's romantic," she finishes.

I smile. It *is* romantic. I have an international lover in the middle of a war zone. I should write a book.

The Greek waiter drops off our food. We smile him off.

"He just acts so flaky all the time. He keeps coming and going. Honestly, half the time I don't even know if he still likes me," I admit.

I glance at the table next to us. There's a little old lady sitting all alone eating her matza ball soup. Most likely that will be me in thirty years. I sigh.

"Maybe you just need to give him more time. His life is so incredibly difficult. We can't even imagine."

I can, but I don't interrupt.

"The same rules don't apply, I think," she continues, stabbing a bite of coleslaw.

"I know, Catherine. I know. It's just so hard. I don't know how much leeway to give him."

"I guess as much as you feel you can or want to." She pauses and then asks, "Do you still love him?"

I pause, wishing I could lie. "Yes. Unfortunately, yes." And I take a big, greasy bite of my grilled cheese, hoping the comfort food comforts me.

* * *

This is what you signed up for Kim. Why are you surprised? I am beginning to wonder if Omar is intentionally sabotaging us. Omayyad. Because that's what it sometimes feels like — sabotage from the inside. As if he's desperate to ruin what is good and real, desperate to destroy any faith I have in him or us.

I'm sitting at my desk, the late winter New York snow falling outside in huge mocking flakes. I try to dig back into the edits I am supposed to be doing on my play, trying to focus. Fail. I can't stop thinking about Omar and look at the notification bar, waiting for it to do tricks or something, to at least show me a damn IM. Seriously, how could he do this? He knows how hurt and pissed off I was last time. There is no way he's doing this again.

Yup. He is doing this again. He is blowing me off *again*. He better be dead again. It's about the only excuse I'll take now.

I just don't get it. When I first returned, some people worried that he was perhaps only after a green card. It's times like these I want to point out to them and say: if he just wanted a green card, he is sure not going about it in a good way! In fact, this is the worst attempt at a green card ever! So clearly he's not after citizenship, not that I ever thought he was. But clearly he's also not after me, as clearly I thought he was.

I look for the 95th time at the online status notification on my Yahoo bar. No Omar. Unbelievable. Is this real? Was anything real?

My cat hops on my lap and meows loudly at me. "I know, Skitty. This sucks. He sucks."

*　　*　　*

IM Mar 31, 2010

02:20:00 PM k: Ok. What in the world is going on? Why do you never pick up your phone? Don't disappear on me again. Please.

08:21:47 PM k: Omar I just heard about the bad bombings in Baghdad. I'm worried. Nothing else matters. Hope your family is all ok.

11:52:40 PM o: famly ok kim thank you

*　　*　　*

'I need to make a change in my thinking.' I am lying on my bed, reading what I wrote recently in my journal. I have been doing a lot of re-reading of my journal lately. Oscar Wilde said he always carries his diary with him on the train because "One should always have something sensational to read." Point taken, Oscar.

I email Omar telling him that since he never keeps appointments with me and can't help but disappear on me, I need to things to change and we need to just be friends. We should take some time apart. It's probably what he always wanted anyway. I feel like I am forcing a relationship in which he is, for whatever reason, incapable.

Three weeks pass, and I don't hear from him. Three weeks. So I guess I was right.

'A relationship with Omar is impossible.' That's another doozy from my journal. Man, I'm going through a lot of journals with Omar. Oscar would be proud.

*   *   *

How is it possible that we care this much about baseball?

I am in a one-act play festival in New Jersey about baseball. Yes, baseball. About fifty people have devoted their time and energy and money to write or direct or design or produce or act in a play about baseball. I am one of them. It feels ridiculous. Does anyone know there are refugees dying? I mean, really. Dying! They are dying waiting for help and we're laughing about baseball. It seems so inane. What is wrong with us?

I come here every day, out to stupid New Jersey. With my own play in a holding pattern, I thought it was important I took on a different creative project having nothing to do with refugees. Well...I found it! And it's ridiculous.

And now I am angry. Who the hell cares about baseball? Omar or no Omar, there are refugees waiting for help—hungry, lost, crying, abandoned. It's ridiculous. This festival is ridiculous. Baseball is ridiculous. Everything not related to refugees seems ridiculous and a waste of time.

I wonder if I should see a therapist.

*　　*　　*

IM Apr 27, 2010

05:22:05 AM o:　<ding> kim?

01:12:33 PM k:　hi omar. I saw you dinged me earlier.

01:12:53 PM o:　hi kim

01:13:16 PM o:　do u have cam

01:13:21 PM o:　i want see u

01:13:28 PM k:　ok hang on turnign on cam

01:13:58 PM o:　waw butefol girl

`01:14:08` PM `k`: please omar don't. don't say that, things are different now

`01:15:21` PM `o`: do u see me?

`01:16:04` PM `k`: yes, your hair is shorter

`01:16:32` PM `o`: and your hair is longer

`01:16:49` PM `k`: yes

`01:17:26` PM `o`: im soory

`01:18:27` PM `o`: haw can one person stay with somebody lake me?

`01:18:46` PM `k`: Omar.

`01:18:59` PM `k`: I don't know. I don't know what to say

`01:19:07` PM `o`: dont say any thing

`01:23:19` PM `o`: u make me shy

`01:23:39` PM `k`: what did you want to say omar?

`01:23:44` PM `o`: i want kiss u

`01:23:55` PM `k`: no don't say those things. we can't go there again omar.

`01:24:09` PM `o`: ok

`01:24:10` PM `k`: we can only be friends now.

`01:24:14` PM `o`: yes

`01:24:21` PM `o`: im soory

`01:24:28` PM `k`: my emotions are too close for that kind of talk

`01:24:46` PM `k`: I will fall for you all over again. And I can't. You keep hurting me. Friends only.

`01:24:47` PM `o`: Oh kim.

`01:24:55` PM `k`: It's the truth Omar

`01:25:09` PM `k`: Say something. Pleaaaase.

01:25:33 PM o: what is that you drink? wisky? ☺

01:25:39 PM k: no, water

01:25:45 PM o: I know kim. I just try make joke

01:25:41 PM o: kim u see me? cam frozen.

01:25:48 PM k: No I can't see u. Oh my god, this is impossible.
Why is this so hard?

*   *   *

"Oh Omar! The painting you sent me is beautiful! It's of us!" I had just opened a package from the Syrian post—a painting from Omar. I can't believe I got a package from Syria! Syria!

"Did you see?" he asks.

"Yes! I can't believe you sent me a painting from Syria! It's beautiful! So beautiful." I hold up the painting in front of me, mesmerized.

"Do you like?"

Do I like. It was us, our first night together laying on his living room floor on his thin little roll-up mattress. It was us, holding each other, wrapped in each other, lost in each other. It was us, crying. It was us and like my mood, it was all blues.

"I love it." I say. I really do. I start to cry. "It's our first night together, Omar."

"Yes, Kim."

"I move the phone away from my mouth. I'm not sure if I want him to know I'm crying. He always promised me a painting. He promised he would paint something special for me. And somehow, miraculously, here I am holding it. He followed through with something. He did this for me.

"I love it, Omar. It's beautiful. Thank you." I say, as I lay the painting on my table, standing back to get some distance, from everything.

"Are you crying, Kimmy?"

"It's ok. It's a good cry." I can't stop looking at the painting. It was all real. I was there. He held me. We were real. I have proof. I didn't make this all up. And all this makes me cry some more.

"Oh habibti, I so sorry." Omar responds helplessly.

"No, Omar. It's perfect. It's absolutely perfect. I love it." The proof of Omar terrifies me. I don't know what to do.

"Baby, habibti…" he says, trying to comfort me from so far.

"I should go Omar. I need to go, I think." I say desperate to get off the phone.

"Kim, I feel I am there with you."

If only he was.

* * *

IM June 15, 2010

05:12:27 PM k: your smile is so beautiful. I like looking at you.

05:12:39 PM o: so

05:12:41 PM k: so

05:12:44 PM k: no more smiling, got it?

05:12:45 PM k: ☺

05:13:17 PM o: i lake your hear

05:13:24 PM k: hair ☺ I can't believe you have internet at home. So much better for us!

05:13:27 PM o: yes, but only for 1 month

05:13:36 PM o: may i ask

05:13:38 PM k: yes?

05:13:58 PM o: 2 questsen

05:14:04 PM k: ok go ☺

05:14:33 PM o: what is that cloth?

05:14:52 PM k: this?

05:14:59 PM k: it's a sweatshirt!

05:14:59 PM o: ahhh

05:15:03 PM k: don't like? ☺

05:15:12 PM o: no no its nice

05:15:38 PM k: it says new york!

05:15:47 PM o: yes i see

05:15:59 PM k: and question 2?

05:16:50 PM o: ok

05:17:04 PM o: but i feel shy

05:17:18 PM k: after everything??

05:17:42 PM o: do u remember me? im shy

05:18:04 PM k: yes...youre shy ☺

05:18:36 PM k: ok

05:19:24 PM o: what is under your cloth?

05:19:40 PM o: your sweat shert

05:19:50 PM k: nothing--- my friend! ☺

05:20:12 PM o: im just a kureas

05:20:15 PM k: uh-huh. curious?

05:20:25 PM o: yes that's all

05:20:43 PM k: well...friends shouldn't be so curious about such things with friends ☺

IM June 19, 2010

05:23:27 PM o: i dont open all the lights because a freand is sleeping here

05:23:44 PM o: see? this is the place we sleep before you and me you remember?

05:24:53 PM k: yes of course I remember Omar. How could I forget?

05:26:50 PM k: ☺

05:26:55 PM o: my fraend he is here visiting me

05:27:14 PM k: friend from Iraq?

05:27:22 PM o: yes

05:27:28 PM k: what did you tell him about me?

05:27:56 PM o: not evry thing

05:28:09 PM k: so what did you say to him? I'm curious...

05:28:22 PM o: Friends shouldn't be so corious. ☺

05:28:29 PM k: Not fair! Come on!!!

05:28:34 PM o: he know we are real freands

05:28:55 PM k: oh omar.

05:29:18 PM o: i cant till evry body about all my spichalty

05:29:27 PM k: speciality?

05:29:34 PM o: yes you are my specialty kim

IM June 21, 2010

05:55:11 PM k: r u there?

05:55:35 PM o: yes

05:57:35 PM o: whats up

05:57:42 PM k: You know that phrase—what's up??? Funny

05:57:49 PM o: of corse ☺

05:58:00 PM k: whats up! You're already so American-ized! Lord
help me!

05:58:07 PM o: hhhhhhh ☺

05:58:22 PM k: whats up dude?!

*   *   *

It's hot out and I'm having coffee at my local coffee place,
lost in Omarland—a place I frequent in my mind—when I
get an idea: What if I tried to sell Omar's art here? I mean,
why not. I know people who care about things. And I'm in
New York—art central! I bet I could sell some art, some
refugee art. I could send him the money somehow and help
him survive.

"I could do this," I apparently say rather loudly out loud, as people next to me glance over and clearly wonder who I'm talking to.

I take a sip of my iced latte to look normal again. This could work. (I say silently this time) His paintings are good. I mean, I'm no art connoisseur, but they're really good.

That's it. I'm going into the Iraqi art business.

*   *   *

IM Jun 23, 2010

01:10:52 PM o: i get your text about helping sell my paintings kim
01:11:15 PM o: you all ways want helping me. You are like my gard angel
01:11:44 PM o: thank you kimy habebty you make me happy xoxo

*   *   *

"Your aess still butifol?" I'm lying in my bed with my laptop against my knees, IM-ing with Omar, sans video, late one night. He's a little drunk. I'm a little tired. It's been several weeks since we've spoken. I've been trying to create distance.

"No, it's ugly now. You'd hate my ass now," I respond. "Of course, it's still beautiful! No, wait! You mean my eyes, don't you?"

I'm totally embarrassed. He was not enquiring as to the status of my ass. No. He was merely asking if my *eyes* were still beautiful. My eyes. Come on Kim. You must remember his repeat misspells! Thankfully he didn't quite catch my faux-pas.

"Sorry," I type sheepishly.

"No, I like it," he responds. I no longer have any idea what we are talking about.

"Omar, Omar, Omar," I say after a beat, rolling onto my side, wishing he were next to me.

"Kim, Kim, Kim," he cloyingly responds. Our typing pauses. It's amazing to me how filled texting pauses can actually be. I mean, I suppose there is a chance he dozed off, but I hope he's just as lost in all the thought and emotion as I am. I decide to change the mood.

"Are you painting a lot these days? I have sold three of the paintings you sent me. People like them. I think I can sell more."

"No kim my job here is so bad, no money maybe in near time, I will need to go back to Iraq. I not know yet."

Well, this is news. Can he just go back to Iraq? Is it that easy? Won't he be at risk of getting killed?

"Can you just go back?" I ask.

"Yes I take bus, it is long and not saefe, but its no problem."

"But if it's not safe...?" I interrupt. I am trying not to panic. I don't want him in Iraq. It's too dangerous.

"Kimy, I need to see how Baghdad is," he says, and then, "And I am lonely. I need my family."

Iraq.

* * *

IM Aug 1, 2010

07:11:08 PM k: ok goodnight omar.... good to see you online tonight

07:11:44 PM o: butifol girl

07:12:00 PM k: good night omar.

07:12:17 PM o: may i kiss u

07:12:27 PM k: do you want to kiss me?

07:12:37 PM o: yes and u

07:12:51 PM k: of course I want to kiss you Omar. But here we are back here again. And I'm not sure anything has changed. Nothing seems possible

07:13:03 PM o: I want you here with me now

07:13:38 PM k: I just dont understand you omar

07:14:04 PM o: I know i dont understand me too kim

* * *

I am in the bathroom, crying. I am about to give the first public reading of my play for potential producers.

Someone asked me if it was true, if the story with Omar was true. Yes, I said and weakly smiled. Yes, it's all true. And then I almost cried and bolted, quickly excusing myself.

I'm scared. This has always been *my* story—Omar's and my story. And now I am sharing it with other people. I mean I know I have to. It's part of the gig. But I don't know. It's so deeply personal. Can I? And I have to pretend to be the refugees, as well. I have to tell *their* story too. It's all so much. I lean my hands over the sink, as my knees sink in as well.

There's a knock. "We're ready to start. Kim? You ok?" It's Megan. She saw me leave the room. She knows something is up. She knows how hard this is.

I turn my head towards the door and over my shoulder reply, "Yes, be out in a minute, Megan."

I straighten up, look at myself in the mirror and wipe my tears. I have no choice.

Tell the whole story so that the world may know.

* * *

"It went well. I mean, I told our story and people liked it."

"Yes, Kim," Omar responds. As usual, I'm not entirely sure he understood me.

"Well we should hang up. You're paying for this. It's too expensive," I offer. He rarely calls me and when he does I'm super aware of the minutes.

"Yes, Kim," he repeats.

"Oh and thanks for the birthday email and message. Meant a lot."

"Yes, habibti," he says.

"And that picture you sent of me from that day in the mosque wearing the hijab is sooo funny! I look like an old Arab woman!" I start to laugh, even though he feels distant today, far way.

"Yes, like my mom."

"I look like your mom?" I guffaw. "Like your mom in my hijab?"

"Yes, Kim."

Lord help us.

*   *   *

IM Aug 12, 2010

12:56:58 AM o: nace pits
12:58:42 AM k: arm pits???
12:58:45 AM o: yes
12:58:51 AM k: nice arm pits?
12:58:59 AM k: oh my Gawddddd!
12:59:08 AM k: you make me laugh!!

```
12:59:20 AM  k:  oh my god. why are you in my life omar??? Why?
                 ☺
12:59:27 AM  o:  i dont know ☺
12:59:28 AM  k:  this is so crazy. Everything going on in your world
```
and the craziness between us and Syria and we're

discussing my arm pits!

```
12:59:54 AM  k:  you are crazy
01:00:05 AM  o:  u r sexy
01:00:33 AM  o:  i want do sex naw
01:00:42 AM  o:  with u
01:00:47 AM  k:  Thanks for clarifying ☺
01:01:07 AM  o:  stay
01:02:09 AM  o:  u want see my penos?
01:02:15 AM  k:  Stop!!!
```

IM Aug 14, 2010

```
03:25:23 PM  k:  omar
03:25:26 PM  o:  yes
03:25:29 PM  k:  what do we do?
03:25:31 PM  k:  what do I do?
03:25:40 PM  k:  just look at each other I guess
03:26:16 PM  k:  we need to just be friends!!!
03:26:26 PM  k:  right?
03:26:27 PM  o:  more
03:26:39 PM  o:  more
03:26:40 PM  k:  how?
03:27:18 PM  o:  i mean we r more than just freands
```

`03:27:28 PM k:` Omar please don't hurt me again

`03:28:08 PM o:` im so sory i will never do that agean

`03:28:53 PM k:` dont ok?

`03:28:57 PM o:` ok

`03:29:03 PM k:` just show up and tell me what you need to tell me

`03:29:08 PM k:` but don't not show up

* * *

I hang up the phone. He just said to come to Damascus. He said to come now. I said, are we ready? Should I come? He said yes. I said honestly? He said yes. I said maybe November after my play closes. He said now. I can hardly breathe. Now. He wants me now in Damascus. I think I'm going to Damascus.

I better start applying for a visa.

* * *

"Kim, please," Omar weakly defends himself. He has missed yet another online appointment we had.

"I just don't know why you don't show up, Omar! It drives me crazy! We say noon, noon comes and goes and no Omar!" I am angry...again. Always angry at him lately. I'm continually disappointed in him.

"Kim, I..." he tries to explain. But I know he has nothing to say. He never does.

I am hovering over a windowsill in my living room seeking cell reception, consequently sharing my anger with the whole neighborhood. I am late for a rehearsal for my play. I have to go. I shouldn't have called him right now. I was just so mad. I am about to hang up.

"Kim, remember all those refugees you met in Middle East? I am one of them."

That cut to the quick. I stop the crazy chaos I've been spinning and sit on the wide arm of my favorite orange chair. I *always* remember he's a refugee. No, that's not true. Sometimes I forget he's a refugee. God, he's right. He has had the same experiences, has the same fears, the same depression, the same feelings of futility, the same frustrations. I forgot. He's not like any other man I have ever known. Ever. He is completely different. And so is this relationship.

He continues. "Some days I have no money for internet, Kim. And I don't want tell you that. Some days internet is out. This is Syria, remember? Some days, I so depressed I can't leave my home. I don't want talk to no one—not even my mother or you. So please try remember: *I* am one of those refugees you met."

* * *

It's late. I'm lying in my bed waiting for my neighbors above me to finish having sex so I can sleep. And I can't stop looking at the painting Omar made of us, conveniently hung next to my bed—our first night together, all blues and shadows. He's so good. He's such a good artist. He captured our expressions perfectly: me looking at him madly in love, his arm across my stomach, him looking slightly down, looking…what is that expression? Out of reach? Hmm, is that accurate? Was he out of reach? Is he out of reach?

The romantic ruckus above me stops. I roll over to my other side to try to sleep. He's always been out of my reach, hasn't he? He's never been fully 100% committed. I have always been the instigator of this relationship. God, is that true? Did he paint the truth? Shit. I don't like this new discovery. Visa in place, tomorrow I am planning to buy my ticket to Damascus. No time for these thoughts. I roll onto my stomach and try to sleep.

*　　*　　*

Boobididoop ting!

My phone alerts me to a text. I am focused on my study guide from the beginning Arabic language class I enrolled in, determined to share a language with Omar, but nonetheless give a cursory glance to my phone. It's Omar!

Yay! Unexpected text from Omar. I can practice my Arabic! Yay! I didn't expect to hear from him. This means he's finally initiating conversations with me. All is well in the world! Al-hamdulillah! (That means "Praise God." Kim's Arabic Dictionary 795th installment.)

"Kim. Can't come online today. Sorry. I met Iraqi girl. I think I love her. Am happy."

I sit there frozen at my desk reading that text, over and over and over again. I read that text so many times, I think my eyes will break. 'I met Iraqi girl. I think I love her. Am happy.' Iraqi girl? Love? Am happy? What the? Remember *me*? Your supposed on-again-off-again *girlfriend*. I guess we're off-again. Are you kidding me? What is happening right now? Did I just get broken up with via an international text? Did I just pay thirty cents to have my heart smashed?

I am so shocked by this cavalier text, and the improbability of receiving such hurtful news via this form that it takes a while for the waterworks to start, but they eventually do of course. I am a girl after all. I start to pace, not knowing what else to do. And then my knees surrender and down I go. Floor. Knees. Down. And for the rest of the night, I am on the floor.

Many, many hours later, with no other communication from Omar, I pick myself off the floor, shake off the cat hair and cancel my reservation for Damascus. How did I let this happen? Again?

Two months pass before I speak with Omar again.

*   *   *

I look around the simple dining hall, listening to the clinking of the silverware during the silent evening meal. It's just me and fifteen monks. I start to silently laugh. Omar drove me to a monastery! Not literally, of course. That would involve me actually *seeing* Omar again. No, no. I took a train, but Omar drove me here indeed. So here I am at a monastery as their sole guest this weekend. Just me and the monks.

I decided to retreat to this monastery for three days to think, pray, listen, meditate and hopefully, heal. Screw it. Truth is I need to get over Omar. I needed to do something after that last brutal break-up. For some reason, a monastery in New Jersey sounded about right.

The monk who picked me up at the train station looked deceivingly like a civilian. Trickster! Apparently, monks do not need to be in monk robes at all times. They are apparently allowed to wear Midwestern-looking shorts, Nike t-shirt, socks and sandals.

"Welcome. We hope you find peace here," the casually dressed monk said to me after our brief introductions in front of the sedan. Chatty, he is not.

"Me too. Is it guaranteed?" I wanted to ask. "Will I get my money back if I haven't figured it all out by Monday morning?" But instead, I smile, embrace the silence and look at the lovely scenery opening up in front of me. Who knew New Jersey was so beautiful?

The monastery is located in a wooded area, with creeks, hills, hiking trails and apparently easy access to God—all that for $40 a night. My driver monk surprises me by speaking and pulls me out of my thoughts. He mentions he is about to retire.

"Heading down to Florida."

Wait. Is this legal? Can monks just retire? Can they become civilians and retire to a condo in Florida like the rest of us? How do you go from living a monastic life to a spring break-based existence? I congratulate him, smile again and return to the overwhelming scenery. I am not here to talk.

After settling in to my room, ("Best guest room we have, as you're the only guest.") I explore the grounds— finding an old chapel, a cemetery, trails and plenty of space. I make it back in time for lunch with dessert. ("We have dessert with every meal and many of the monks here are diabetic because of it." Was that annoyance in his voice?) After lunch, I nap, journal, hike some more, meditate on a hill and cry. During evening vespers, ("Please don't sing too loudly. It disturbs the monks.") I study my songbook, the cross, the monks dressed in monk-ly brown robes finally(!) and my own soul—anything and everything to figure out why I am here in this monastery and this mess with Omar.

The service ends. Not wanting to disturb the monk-ly routine, I wait for a cue to stand. My retiring driver monk gestures to me at last, and we are off to monk happy hour before the evening meal. Yes, monk happy hour. Monks drink. Again, who knew?

And after this first day, after drinking my cheap red leftover communion wine and after eating a huge meal and my diabetes-causing chocolate cake made by holy hands in the nearby kitchen, I send up a prayer for peace. Or something.

*   *   *

I am meandering down my street today in upper Manhattan. It's a beautiful day and I am on my way home from my yoga class. I'm back in yoga and it feels good. I need to keep doing self-care.

Now I will admit I have yoga head, but am more clear-headed than as of late, determined to keep the peace I found in the monastery, when a really cute guy walks by. I notice him. Huh. Today is the first time I have noticed a cute man since Omar. I think I forgot there were other men in the world. I look at him. Cute, indeed. Very cute. He is walking with a woman (of course), talking to her... in English. English! Here is my strange thought of the day: "Wow. How easy it would be to date him. He speaks English and lives on this continent." Isn't that crazy? This is what I think.

I have to get home to work on projects, but I stop to watch the couple until they turn the corner and disappear. How easy it would be if only I fell in love with *this* guy who lives on my street and speaks English. But I didn't. I fell for Omar. Not that it matters anymore. After all — 'met Iraqi girl, am happy'.

For God's sake, who says that?

* * *

"I don't know how you do this play night after night, Kim," Megan stops to tell me as I'm packing up my bag for the night. It has been a long day, but a good show. We are in the middle of a performance run in New York for my play I finally finished writing about Omar and the other three million refugees.

I am grateful and exhausted, on every level. She knows. She was there. She knows the emotional stakes for me in telling this story—this story I wrote and lived, especially considering the current state of things, the current state of Omar.

"I don't know, Megan. It's not how I imagined it to be, that's for sure!"

She gives me a hug and a smile and I run to catch my train.

It's not how I imagined it would be.

*   *   *

Omar keeps private messaging me. I keep ignoring him. Let him ping his Iraqi girlfriend! Literally! Ping you, Omar. I'm too tired for this. Randy, Catherine and of course my mom all say walk away. I am trying. But every night onstage, I have to talk about how great he is. It's not easy. In fact, it's kind of hard.

It's been over two months since we have spoken. I am justifiably heartbroken and justifiably mad. I mean, up until the "I met Iraqi girl. I think I love her. Am happy" text, I was ready to move to Damascus to be with him. Literally.

"How long should I come to Damascus for?" I asked. "Forever," he answered. We laughed. Forever! Okay! Forever! On my way! I remember that conversation so well. Too well. "Forever!" Lord help me. I was his. He was mine. End of story. And then—enter Iraqi girl. Dun dun dun! How could I compete? She's there—with him, like my cute American on the street in my neighborhood. Easy! And she's Iraqi! I surrender!

And here is Omar, eagerly trying to talk to me again. Why is he in hot pursuit now? Part of me of course is curious. But I don't care, or rather I *try* not to care.

He texts me. He emails me. He messages me. "Please, Kim, I am sorry, Kim. Are you there, Kim? Please, Kim." Blah, blah, blah. Screw it. Screw him. Ping him. Ping off! I'm not doing this again. Not now.

I *did* fall for the wrong Iraqi. He was right.

Ignore. Sign out. Ma'asalaama.

*   *   *

His relationship ended with the Iraqi. Almost seems inconsequential now. What is important and telling, was that he was willing to *start* it. But funny thing, turns out all they had in common was their "Iraq-ness". It was over within a few weeks of beginning. Surprise, surprise.

"Please understand, Kim. She Iraqi. Everyone say it is better as refugee if I married. Everyone say 'get married' and better to marry Iraqi. Looks better to agency. And then I meet this girl and she is nice," Omar tells me after I finally relented and answered one of his calls. "Please understand."

"Omar, stop. Enough. I was coming to Damascus to visit you and you broke my heart. How could you do that to me?"

"Please, Kim." It sounds as if he is almost crying, "I don't know what to do. I am so alone here." I am reminded of Raheel, my smoking alley man with the family in Iowa. "I am so alone here," Raheel cried. My brain whirls. How many displaced Iraqis have said these words since the invasion?

Call me crazy, call me naïve, but in some messed-up way, I understand. I sympathize. I've heard too many stories not to. He thought he should be married to an Iraqi, that it would in some way help and so he tried.

It's tricky being a refugee. So many more considerations than we can imagine. The rules are different. The rules I would apply to my imaginary American street boyfriend don't work here. Omar has to think about what *looks* best. He is living virtually *illegally* as a refugee waiting for resettlement. Image is everything.

His story is his passport out. And if everyone says having an Iraqi wife will help him get out, then of course, he looks for an Iraqi wife. I understand! Then again, I'm overly understanding. I wonder if I love him more than he loves me.

I tell him I don't know what to say, that I don't know how to proceed and if I even *want* to proceed. We hang up and I proceed to think about him nonstop. We proceed to text the next day. And the next. I proceed to call him the next week and again a few days after that and again and again. I try to keep my distance, to stay cautious—I'm no fool. But apparently I am, because after not that much time passes, we seem to be right back there again, back where we've always been: acting as more than we are. Why can I not stop this man? It's like an addiction. I think I'm addicted to Omar.

"I miss you Kim, beautiful Kim," he says, as I'm lying on my bed, 6 p.m. my time, 1 a.m. his time, our bewitching hour, the perfect time in our schedules for both of us to talk.

"Go to sleep, Omar. And try not to dream of me."

"What you mean, Kim? I not understand," he says, sleepily.

"Never mind. Not important. I miss you too. Good night, sweet Omar."

I press end, look at the phone and sigh. Do not fall in love with him again, Kim. Friends. You are only friends. Be his friend. Stop flirting. He dumped you for another girl. Stop fantasizing about Omar. Get off this bed. Get out of the past. Get a life. Find a man who lives in this city...or at least on this continent.

*   *   *

IM Nov 18, 2010

04:19:20 PM o: what r u doing

04:19:28 PM k: wow

04:19:31 PM k: you're a surprise

04:20:05 PM k: what are you doing?

04:20:13 PM o: drink and eat

04:20:49 PM o: i want see u on cam

04:21:09 PM o: im wisky

04:21:42 PM k: you're always whisky!

04:21:50 PM k: are u drunk?

04:21:52 PM o: yes

04:21:59 PM k: Knew it

04:22:23 PM o: wow look at you

04:22:49 PM k: turn on your cam

04:23:18 PM o: hi

04:23:26 PM o: haw r u you see me?

04:23:28 PM k: yes hi

04:23:42 PM o: butifiol girl

04:23:53 PM k: I'm ok

04:23:59 PM k: feeling a bit lonely tonight

04:24:23 PM o: y?

04:24:32 PM k: you know....

04:24:52 PM o: what?

04:24:58 PM k: i just mean

04:25:04 PM k: im lonely

04:25:22 PM o: oh kimy me too

04:25:29 PM k: I know

04:26:19 PM k: how are u omar?

04:26:31 PM o: Kim

04:27:17 PM k: just talk to me

04:27:45 PM k: how are you? whats going on?

04:31:58 PM o: as u lake

04:32:29 PM k: I just mean...

04:32:33 PM k: What is happening with you? You said you might go back home to visit your family. Is it safe to go back to Baghdad? Is that happening?

04:32:50 PM o: kim

04:33:56 PM o: u still love me?

04:34:48 PM k: probably.

04:34:58 PM k: But I'm trying not to.

04:35:47 PM k: say something

04:36:27 PM k: we can't keep looking at each other like this

04:37:32 PM o: you r butifol

04:37:41 PM k: Oh Omar

IM Dec 9, 2010

12:50:00 PM o: hi kim

12:50:38 PM k: Omar! Finally! Are you in Baghdad?

12:51:04 PM o: gease

12:51:14 PM k: huh?

12:51:30 PM o: gase

12:51:43 PM k: what is that? Gase?

12:52:10 PM o: its english word

12:52:39 PM k: I don't understand you Omar. What is gase?

12:52:52 PM o: it mean can you know what or where?

12:53:45 PM k: Omar. What are you talking about? You're not making sense.

12:53:54 PM k: Just start over.

12:53:59 PM k: are you in Syria?

12:54:04 PM o: ok kim im in Baghdad

12:54:09 PM k: Wow

12:54:13 PM k: Is everything ok?

12:54:51 PM o: i m happy and sad and alot of things

12:55:08 PM k: I bet it's great to be back in some ways

12:55:04 PM o: i miss my home

12:55:12 PM k: of course you do.

12:55:17 PM k: how long will you stay?

12:55:27 PM o: 5 days more and i will be back in syria

12:55:41 PM k: ah I see. are u safe?

12:55:50 PM o: haw r u kim

12:55:58 PM k: Don't worry about me

01:07:39 PM o: can you come to syria?

01:07:49 PM k: What? No omar. Are you kidding me?

01:07:59 PM k: I tried this 2 months ago

01:08:16 PM k: My God! Are you serious?? I can't keep doing this with you. You're killing me!

01:08:16 PM o: but i say ok to come

01:08:23 PM k: but you said ok last time!

01:08:32 PM k: and then you met a girl and told me you loved her and I cried for 3 straight weeks!

01:08:48 PM o: my gad kim

01:09:37 PM k: I was on my way to visit you!

01:09:46 PM k: ...and then you sent me that text.

01:10:12 PM k: and I had to perform my play about how much I loved you every night.

01:11:09 PM o: i shold go naw

01:11:12 PM k: Are u kidding me Omar? You want to go now? This is ridiculous. Yup ok. Goodbye.

*   *   *

"Waleed has exebishon in US soon kim. Texas. We are 6 artist. And he can send invetashn for two persons to come to US," Omar told me on Yahoo Messenger one day.

"Wow. Will you go?" I coolly type, as my heart races. Omar here?

"Maybe."

"Good for you, Omar." Not getting involved. Not getting involved. Not getting involved. "I hope it is successful for you."

"If i come can you see me?"

I hesitate. Can I see him? My dream for the past two years. Omar in the U.S. and can I see him, he asks.

"I will try," I stupidly answer.

"Way you say it like that?"

Why do I say it like that? Let me count the ways...

"Omar, you know why."

"Oh, Kim."

"Plus Texas is far from me. But I will try. I just can't get too excited. I just can't allow myself to imagine things."

"Kimy..."

"But yes, I will try." There is a long pause. And with no cam, I no longer know how to read our pauses. "Omar? Are you there?" I type.

"Sorry kim i cant fikes too much."

"Fikes?" I ask.

"No, fox. Foxes!"

I start to laugh. "OMG. What are you talking about, Omar? What are you saying?"

"Oh kim you are my best freand."

"Oh, Omar, no I'm not." I hesitate. How I want this. Him. "I'm just a girl you met once in Damascus."

"Please kim I cant foxes now with you."

"OMG. I don't know what you mean by foxes, Omar!! But ok just go. I'll text you later."

I end the connection and sit there. Omar in Texas. O.M.Y.

Oh! Focus! He couldn't focus! That was the word! He was trying to say *focus*!

Foxes. Hysterical.

As usual, communication failure.

*　　*　　*

IM Dec 22, 2010

12:09:52 PM o: u look sad kim

12:10:25 PM k: i guess I am a little sad .... but it's ok. I was glad to see you online tonight

12:10:50 PM k: Why is Alaa there with you?

12:11:15 PM o: we are friends and im alone i need some budy with me

12:11:34 PM k: r u ok?

12:11:43 PM o: no but its ok

12:11:54 PM k: tell me

12:15:11 PM o: can i go knaw?

12:15:37 PM k: I dont know why you dont talk to me, why you always run away from me

12:17:29 PM o: may i go?

12:17:38 PM k: no Omar.

```
12:17:43 PM o: yes

12:17:48 PM k: I call I message. You never respond!

12:18:37 PM k: fine go

12:18:39 PM o: oh kim

12:18:46 PM k: this is too hard. You're a child.
```

IM Dec 29, 2010

```
04:06:00 PM o: <ding>

04:06:27 PM k: Hello Omar.

04:07:08 PM o: hi kim

04:07:14 PM o: I just want say next thirsday i ll go to UN

04:07:24 PM o: to ask about my sitchwashon

04:07:31 PM k: ok

04:07:55 PM o: alot of my freands go

04:08:01 PM k: go where?

04:08:07 PM k: leaving syria?

04:08:23 PM o: yes imegrashon

04:08:26 PM k: I see

04:08:29 PM k: what do you want?

04:08:45 PM o: i want leave

04:09:10 PM k: omar

04:08:45 PM o: I want kiss u

04:09:16 PM k: Omar. stop.

04:09:31 PM o: i know

04:09:42 PM k: you want me until you can have me...and then you
                dont want me.

04:09:45 PM o: u r raght
```

04:09:53 PM k: so tell me what to do.

04:10:02 PM k: its not fair to me

04:10:02 PM o: not naw

04:10:07 PM k: why?

04:10:28 PM o: t want tame to explan

04:10:39 PM k: I need you to explain now.

04:10:39 PM o: and naw i want go

04:10:49 PM k: always the same

04:11:09 PM o: sorry kime plese

04:11:16 PM k: you are going to lose me

04:11:28 PM o: no

04:11:19 PM o: dont be ingree

04:11:28 PM k: Im not angry omar just tired

04:11:29 PM o: no

04:11:35 PM k: tired of the same over and over

04:13:13 PM o: kim i want live my lafe like all the humens

04:13:20 PM k: I want that too

04:13:23 PM k: for you omar

04:13:33 PM k: I want you to have a normal life

04:14:41 PM o: haw can i fixe us

*   *   *

"Omar, listen. I'm killing myself over here. If you want me, you have to fight for me. I can't keep fighting for both of us." I am pulling at a random loose thread on my favorite orange chair in my New York living room. Since I get the best phone reception while sitting in this chair, I sit here a lot talking to Omar. It has been over two years since we were in the same room. I have learned the tricks to the trade.

"Omar, if you feel strongly about me, you must do something!" There is a long pause. I worry we were disconnected again. It always happens. Damn Syria. Damn Yahoo. Damn Omar. I'm so sick of all of this! But then Omar quietly responds, "There is nothing in my hand to do."

I don't care. I just want him to call me more or email me more or commit to me more, something! Anything! But he never sees it that way and nothing changes.

"You know my situation, Kim. I am refugee." He is right. Damn it, he is right! He is a refugee—all power stripped away by the very fact he has no legal status, no job, no country, no foreseeable future. He is separated from his family, his homeland, his culture, his past—stuck in this *present* that offers him nothing and a *future* he is not allowed to imagine.

Sometimes I think he is simply unable to *imagine* a future with me. How can he imagine? Like so many of the Iraqis I have met, he's been forced to stop imagining, stop dreaming. The only thing you have is today and you hope a car bomb or a kidnapping doesn't take *that* away. My country, his country—they're both guilty. We're all guilty.

But unlike him, I live in the land of imagination, of freedom—the U. S. of A. I believe *anything* is possible. I live freely, work freely, and travel freely. I expect safety. I expect possibility. I expect the fulfillment of my dreams. He neither expects nor imagines any of it. He is just trying to stay alive.

This is perhaps the greatest crime in our nations' criminal acts and the greatest difference between Omar and me. It's not the culture, or the history between our countries or even the war that causes the chasm between us. It's that he does not believe—no, he cannot believe. Just like the children I met on the mountain top center that refused to dream. They have all been taught through experience *not* to believe, not to dream. Omar doesn't believe and I cannot believe for both of us much longer. That thought makes me so sad, I have to hang up, curl into my big orange chair and cry.

Three Visas

"So how is it in Syria these days? The news says people are protesting." I am Skyping on the computer with Omar. Skype now apparently works better in Syria. But I'm Skyping quietly as I am at my mom's house and she doesn't entirely approve of this relationship, really never has.

"Yes, Kim," Omar responds simply.

"Are any Iraqis protesting?"

"Not yet," he responds.

Omar is quiet today. Some days he is sad. This must be one of those days.

"Are you safe?" I ask. These days, that is always my concern. Watching the sensational 24-hour news cycle here is enough to cause sufficient fear.

"Yes, Damascus is still safe for now." For now. For how long, I wonder? I want him out of there.

I hear my mom milling about. I keep quiet. I don't want her to worry. Ever since I've returned from the Middle East, she worries about me—perhaps rightfully so. After all I am in love with an Iraqi refugee who has repeatedly broken my heart. She's not far off base with her concern.

"Is your family okay, Omar?"

"Yes, Kim. Thank you. They are all well. My mother says to send you her greetings," he mentions. My mom never sends hers. Although occasionally I send fake ones.

"Thanks, Omar. That's nice." There is a bit of an awkward pause. Sometimes I don't know where I stand with this man. It's impossible actually—most of the time.

"Well, I should go, Omar."

"As you wish, Kim."

*   *   *

IM Feb 27, 2011

01:51:13 PM o: Are you mad kim?

01:52:23 PM k: I'm not mad omar. Just cautious. I don't know

01:53:44 AM o: kim

01:54:29 AM o: you stay inside me

01:56:11 AM o: yesterday i cry thinking theer is somebody in the world lake you

01:56:18 AM k: oh omar...

01:56:47 AM o: dont forgeat me please

*   *   *

Three Visas

"Maybe you should just go see him," Randy announces one day, as we're walking down 9th Avenue. "Just go and see what is what. It seems as though that's the only way you'll ever know."

Just randomly go and see him, huh? Interesting thought.

*   *   *

"Kim, I am leaving Syria very soon. It's not good here anymore." Omar tells me one day on the phone, as I was getting ready to leave my apartment and rather soon the country.

"Wait, what?" It was just weeks before I was planning to visit him in Syria—to heed Randy's advice and finally just go. Omar doesn't know. I intended it to be a surprise. I was just going to show up and see what happened. No expectations this time. No disappointments. Just answers.

"Wait, so you're actually leaving? When did this happen? When will you be back?" I am starting to panic. I somehow got my visa accepted and was going to buy the ticket today or tomorrow. I have the Travelocity and Expedia windows open on my desktop. I am basically on my way to see him again after all these years of effort and now this—what, a revolution?

189

"Kim, we are not safe here, very bad for Iraqi. You know that. I go with a friend back to Baghdad in maybe in three days."

With the Syrian/Iraqi border still open many Iraqis travel back and forth to Baghdad to assess the violence and see which city is safer to live in. Omar has traveled back and forth across the border by bus twice since I've known him. It's not particularly safe, but there are not a lot of options. And the wish, of course, despite what the ignorant of the world think, is always to be able to return home. Omar is apparently once again assessing the situation in Iraq to see if he can do just that: return home. I just didn't expect him to be doing this now, not when I'm finally coming to visit him on a surprise trip to Syria. Unbelievable.

"I have to tell you. Omar. I can't believe this is happening. I was planning on coming to see you next month. I was planning on coming—to finally see you," I confess. My confession is met with silence.

"Oh, Kim. It not good now. You know this. Syria is not so safe—for both of us." He's right of course. It's dangerous for an Iraqi and for an American and probably more dangerous for an Iraqi with an American.

"And I don't know how long I stay in Iraq. Maybe long time. I not know, Kim."

Three Visas

I can't believe I'm being thwarted from seeing Omar again by a freakin' civil war. Not to be all me me me, but are you serious? Is the universe *conspiring* to keep us apart? Is this the big sign I've been waiting for?

For months now, I have been begging 'please God, send me a sign.' And now survey says... A REVOLUTION! Or is it a *revelation*? That thought gives me pause.

The window of time that I could travel in is now. I have an opportunity to go with a group from an American non-profit. I wouldn't have to go alone, which would be safer and make my mom happier. This opportunity isn't two months from now. It's now. *Now* is the window for me to go. And really, let's be honest: Syria probably isn't going to get better anytime soon. It's probably only going to get more dangerous. So waiting really isn't an option. And *now* is when Omar decides it's time to go back to Baghdad. What timing. I mean, I know there are bigger issues at stake here than my little love story—but *really*, Syria?

"Kim I should go now. I am scared to talk on phone, you know...Syria. We can talk soon online. Okay Kim? I sorry, Kim. There is nothing in my hands to do."

And like that he's gone again. I hesitate and then start to pack up my purse and bag. A revolution. Seriously?

*   *   *

IM Mar 21, 2011

05:17:00 PM k: So what's going on?

05:17:18 PM o: oh u know... middle east

05:17:31 PM k: Ha.

05:17:49 PM k: I'm worried. News here is crazy. Is Damascus safe?

05:18:01 PM o: no its not

05:18:06 PM k: explain

05:18:23 PM k: whats going on?

05:18:45 PM o: people here look at me difrent than befor

05:19:04 PM o: i feel im like a spy

05:19:11 PM k: Oh Omar

05:20:33 PM o: i dont know what will happen in the future its no good here

05:24:50 PM o: its a revoluoshin here

05:27:30 PM o: everybody waiting to get out

05:27:19 PM k: do you still want to come to US?

05:27:35 PM o: yes but haw?

05:28:09 PM k: I'm not sure. Let me think.

*   *   *

"I have to do something to help him, Randy," I say. "Even if we don't end up together. I have to. And an artist visa would at least get him in the country."

I know Randy thinks I'm nuts. All my friends do. And as my best friend, Randy is more worried than most. Omar has been the never-ending story that brings his best friend nothing but tears. We are standing in a small gallery in the heart of the art district in New York City. The gallery owner has agreed to allow me to hold a solo exhibition here in January for Omar. This will do just fine, indeed. Omar will have an exhibit.

"One more question: do you offer possible artist visas for foreign artists?" I ask/slash/pray.

Lisa, the gallery owner, apologizes; that's not part of the deal. Sigh. A gallery, but no visa; same old story. Ever since Waleed's tentative show for the six Iraqi artists fell through, I have been wracking my brain trying to find a way to get Omar an artist visa to get him into the country. I have been desperately seeking an art venue that might be able to sponsor him—not an easy task. No one is interested in taking on the burdens or costs of a visiting international artist from Iraq. I've hopped from gallery to gallery, but shows are scheduled two years out and artist visas are apparent pipe dreams.

Lawyers have told me, "If you get an artist visa, whatever you do, don't lie and don't overstay the visa". Colleagues in the non-profit/humanitarian world have told me, "It's best to wait for a resettlement visa if you can get one from the U.S." And my friends say, "You're doing what now for Omar?"

Errgh! We need a visa. Period. The U.S. resettlement program is extremely backlogged and extremely inefficient. Hundreds of thousands of refugees wait fruitlessly for years, their lives on the line every day, and still getting nowhere. Omar is on that list, but as a single male, how long will he have to wait? As a single male, he is not a priority. An artist visa would at least get him into safety and out of Syria. So I try.

Randy looks at me. "What do you think Kim? Still wanna do it?" He and Lisa await my answer.

I have to do *something*. Things are getting bad in Syria. Omar needs out, but first he needs money. An unmentioned side effect of a brewing civil war is that no one is interested in buying things—like art. They are focused on other things—like food. In short, Omar is broke. I need to help him sell his art.

"Yes, let's have a show."

I just upped my Iraqi art game.

*   *   *

IM Apr 4, 2011

03:10:41 PM o: i want say thank you habebty
03:10:48 PM o: and my famely say helo

Three Visas

03:11:00 PM k: are u ok? You made it to Baghdad ok?

03:11:03 PM o: yes not easy but yes

03:11:09 PM k: please send my greetings

03:11:13 PM k: I see you now! Cam is up. Hi!

03:11:52 PM k: short hair!!

03:12:10 PM k: you're skinny! are u eating enough?

03:12:33 PM o: no im bezy

03:12:54 PM o: lol

03:12:58 PM k: eat more!!

03:13:11 PM k: your mother would say the sam

03:13:15 PM o: She does

03:13:48 PM k: it's good to see you omar,

03:13:48 PM k: was your trip on the bus ok?

03:13:48 PM o: i feel im not on the earth

03:13:53 PM k: what do u mean?

03:13:58 PM o: my god

03:14:08 PM o: i mean fore exampel

03:14:17 PM o: now there is no electricity

03:14:27 PM o: and its so hot

03:14:48 PM o: I feel I am in a strenge place on earth

03:14:59 PM o: you cant imagen it here in bagdad

03:15:04 PM k: oh omar.

03:15:08 PM o: but its ok

03:15:12 PM k: and your family does this, every day

03:15:19 PM o: yes everyone do

03:15:46 PM o: do you know kim the people here

03:15:59 PM o: becose of all thes things are afread

03:16:35 PM o: that theer is no future

03:16:53 PM o: for the next genoration

03:17:13 PM o: no savlisiton

03:17:28 PM k: no salvation?

03:17:44 PM o: yes they are afread there is no salvation

*　　*　　*

Today Omar wished me a happy crustacean day. Well actually "crestaeon day", which turned out to be Christian day, by which he meant Easter. "Congratulations," he said, wishing me "happy Christian day".

For a while, that one was a puzzle on par with "foxes".

*　　*　　*

IM May 1, 2011

10:45:19 AM o: im ok

10:45:25 AM k: just ok? Will you go back to Damascus soon?

10:45:52 AM o: syrea is so bad you know

10:46:35 AM k: what have you heard?

10:46:54 AM o: every budy is wory

10:47:33 AM o: and here in Baghdad i feel more safe and comfortobl

10:47:43 AM k: you do?

10:48:19 AM o: i dont have alot of choises kim

Three Visas

IM May 17, 2011

07:00:54 AM o: hi kim i will go to syrea today with ahmed

07:01:16 AM o: I want to see if i can stay or not if it safe

07:03:00 AM o: This is not life in Baghdad. I cannot live like this

IM May 29, 2011

03:03:10 PM k: You made it.

03:03:15 PM k: So how's Damascus?

03:03:34 PM o: Not good everyone scared

03:03:42 PM o: we all wate

*   *   *

"S.O.S." was what the IM was titled. S.O.S. I came home, opened my Yahoo Messenger, as I always do and this is what popped up.

Omar has never been so dramatic before. He's been scared certainly. He's always scared in Damascus, rightfully so. But never *this* scared or desperate-sounding. In the past, he has said he doesn't know if he's safe. He has said he doesn't know what to do. But never has he used the global maritime distress signal before. Never that. Crap.

IM Jun 4, 2011

10:39:32 AM o: S.O.S. Kim can you email IOM [*International Office of Migration*] and ask them what we Iraqis should do? I'm sorry, but we all scared and alone.

Offices in Damascus all closed because of
violence. I cannot get medical exam for visa. No
more doctors. Should I go Jordan? How we leave?
What we do? Please help. We are stuck here.
Please. S.O.S.

As he and the other twelve bejillion Iraqis await the insanely slow process of possible resettlement in the middle of a revolution, their paperwork often expires. Medical forms become no longer valid. Sometimes the asylum seeker has to go through all the tests and paperwork *again* just to keep their refugee status current. So Omar's medical is no longer current and there are no more doctors in Damascus. Ah! The sweet, simple life of a refugee!

Even though it's a hot New York day, I feel cold as I sit here pondering this IM, trying not to panic. So what can I do in a New York minute? I am in America, thousands of miles away from Damascus. IOM is a huge operation! What good would an email do? Who would I even email? What would I say? "I know someone in Syria stuck and scared. Do you know that? Do you know you have an Iraqi or two stuck in Syria during this apparent civil war?" Of course they know!

A phone call with my mom yielded the advice to pray. Ok, good Lord. Fine mom. But I mean come on! I have to be able to do more than pray, for cry-i! (Nonetheless: God, please help Omar and all the Iraqis get to safety in the middle of this insanity. And help them get their medical exams. The end. Amen.)

Then I start emailing everyone I know in the biz; the refugee biz, that is. It turns out I know *a lot* of people in the refugee world now. I end up writing something close to: "What can we do? The Iraqis are stuck! Omar is stuck! What can we do?" And then, prayers answered in a stroke of divine inspiration, I remember I *do* know someone at IOM. What the? I know someone at IOM! Omar's far-fetched suggestion was no longer so far-fetched. Omayyad! I scrounge my Gmail history for who I know and how, then find her name and email her. Voila! Success! *And* she emails me back!

IM Jun 4, 2011

03:53:02 AM k: Omar! I have information! IOM lady says to email the following address to get advice for you and others. She said they will help and here is the cell phone of a doctor who will open again next week. A cell phone! Call for an appointment! If you can't get the doctor, she said to tell her! Good, yes?

OMY! Good, yes! Call me Annie Sullivan, because I am a miracle worker! I pat myself on the back very hard for my big success: I got much needed refugee information for my friends in Syria. Move over Angelina Jolie! I'm a refugee rock star! I can do anything!

* * *

IM Jun 7, 2011

02:09:41 PM k: So you really want to come to the US Omar?

02:09:56 PM o: i want but haw?

02:10:17 PM o: its not ezey to go us

02:10:41 PM k: I have some ideas but I want to make sure you are ready

02:10:54 PM k: I was talking to Waleed and he thinks maybe you dont want to...

02:11:07 PM o: no i want to

02:11:18 PM k: you werent sure for the last 2 years

02:11:22 PM k: now you want to? For sure?

02:11:28 PM o: yes

02:11:36 PM k: how come?

02:11:53 PM o: i dont know

02:12:32 PM o: i lose all my hope to retorn to iraq

02:12:42 PM k: oh omar

02:12:47 PM o: yes

02:12:53 PM k: I'm sorry

02:13:03 PM k: I know u wanted to return someday

02:13:17 PM o: and serya is not a perfeact plase

02:13:26 PM k: far from it

Three Visas

02:13:47 PM o: yes

02:14:04 PM k: so

02:13:47 PM o: so

02:14:14 PM k: you think you could be happy in U.S?

IM Jun 17, 2011

01:24:36 AM o: do u still love me kimy?

01:24:43 AM k: probably

01:24:50 AM k: do u still love me oomy?

01:26:17 AM o: when i see your eyes now i feel i love this girl and
i feel that i know u from a long time

01:26:27 AM k: me too

01:27:36 AM o: Are u sleepy?

01:26:40 AM k: yes its late

01:27:01 AM o: i want kiss your eyes

01:27:09 AM k: people always ask me if it's true

01:27:22 AM o: what is true

01:27:33 AM k: you. If what I wrote in the play is true, if you are
true

01:28:14 AM k: I tell them it's all true

01:28:41 AM o: its like a leagon

01:28:53 AM k: legend?

01:28:54 AM k: yes

01:29:07 AM o: I'm a legend

01:29:14 AM k: Yes, ☺ but they always ask how does it end

01:28:25 AM k: I say I don't know, we dont know the ending yet.

*　　*　　*

"What is a fiankey, Kim?" Omar asks. It takes me a moment, but I burst out laughing.

I'm on tour in Minneapolis on a lunch break from a rehearsal of my play. I am back in my old home state performing for a week at a Minneapolis theatre. It's wonderful, but my head is heavy with emotions, since I am simultaneously living and acting my relationship with Omar.

Again.

It gets confusing.

It's nice to be laughing together after last night's difficult texts discussing how to get him out of Syria, which left me in tears. I can't manage to secure an artist visa and we're both sick to death of waiting for the U.S. government's regular refugee program to take him. Damascus will fall before that happens. So I offered him something else—another option.

"What's so funny, Kim? What is Fiankey? You write it in your email today."

"*Fiancé*, Omar. A fiancé visa. I was asking you what you would think if we applied for a fiancé visa for you." This conversation might be longer than my thirty-minute break will allow. "That's what I was saying."

Omar is silent.

"Are you there?" I ask.

"Kimy," he says with emotion I can hear. "You make me so happy. You want do this?"

"Of course, Omar!" We are both now crying. "All I have been doing for the past two years is trying to see you again so we could see if this is real and see if we want to pursue this ridiculous relationship. But if Mohammed can't get to the mountain…" Wait, that idiom is based in Islam. How clever of me! Although despite its Islamic roots, it will still go over Omar's basic English. Oh well. Someday I will teach it to Omar. I'm so happy!

Several crew members walk by and smile as they head out of the building to get their lunch. I seem to be having this potentially, completely life-changing discussion in public, in the middle of a lobby. I wave and smile through my tears. The crew must be so confused as to what is truth and what is fiction. Truth be told, so am I.

"You could come here to New York and we could spend some time together and see. We could just finally see 'what's what'. Do you want that Omar?"

"Of course I do Kim. Yes," he pauses, "You save my life…again."

I smile. And exhale. I just want him here. "I just don't know how hard or easy a K1 visa is to get, Omar. I don't really know anything about it except I know it will bring you to safety and to me."

"I sorry, what is K1, Kim?"

"Fiankey," I retort.

We both laugh. This feels good. This feels right. I'll bring Omar here. Instead of me going there, I'll bring Omar here. Oh my God—I will bring Omar here! Maybe we'll get married! That is the expectation with a fiancé visa after all! Omar! Marriage! Fiankey! My stomach does 4.5 Olympic-quality pole-vaults. Holy shit!

"Kim, this is big responsibility for you. Are you sure?" Omar says, pulling me back to reality, to this phone call. He's always worried about me.

"Omar, I love you. I want to help you and I want to see you. Do you want to see me?"

"Yes, of course, habibti. Yes."

I love it when he calls me "habibti". It makes my heart palpitate every time he says it. Whenever he uses it, it means we are back in "that" part of this oh-so-complicated relationship.

"Habibi," I respond, using the correct masculine form, proud of myself for demonstrating skills from my Arabic classes. "This seems to be the only way to get an answer to this relationship. And I'm willing if you are…"

"Oh habibti, shukran, yes." He pauses, then asks as if to confirm, "I come to New York with you?"

"Yes, Omar, yes. You come to New York with me." I look out the window at the Minneapolis skyline. The coffee ground grandma was right. It took a while, but I am engaged. Maybe I need to write a new ending for my play—a happy one.

*   *   *

"I sold one of Jassim's paintings, Omar!" I exclaim into my cell phone, while opening freshly delivered box containing a new round of Iraqi art.

"Oh good, Kim. He will be so happy. Jassim need support his family. Thank you, Kim." Omar is always thankful. He is nothing, if not grateful. And I am happy to help the artists—his community.

I shoo my cat off a painting. They made it this far. Don't wreck them now, Skitty!

How did I become an Iraqi art dealer? I have managed to get Omar a private exhibition at a New York gallery. I have sold dozens of paintings sent from Syria to help support these struggling refugee artists. I have many Iraqi friends in the city and am the local chapter chair of an Iraqi refugee advocacy group. Didn't see this one coming! It's amazing how fast your life can change after a life-changing event.

"I have someone interested in one of yours too, Omar. Cross your fingers!" I suspect he has no idea what finger-crossing would have to do with selling a painting, but I'm too excited about the new paintings to take the time to explain such superstitious expressions.

"Yes, Kim," Omar dutifully responds.

"You are so good, Omar. Truly, so talented. I mean, look at this—gorgeous!" The painting I'm holding is red and blue with various symbols and shapes of women visible through multiple layers and textures. It is thrilling to look at and more thrilling to hold. "I don't know anything about art really, but I know I like yours!"

"Sure you do, Kim. I believe you *do* know. You are true artist. I trust your opinion. And your words make me shy. Shukran. Thank you, Habibti." I am smiling and I think he is smiling as well.

"Is Damascus okay, Omar?"

"No, Kim. Not good. Airplanes fly overhead all day. I not feel safe. Yesterday—three car bombs in my neighborhood. We are all worried." I can hear the worry in his voice. He usually tries to hide it better. "But what can we do?"

"Are you going out much?"

"No, I mostly stay in until I cannot anymore. I need my friends and to drink and to use internet, you know. A human being cannot always be so alone. Not healthy."

I know. I wish I could do more to help him. But I am doing all I can. I am selling his paintings and getting him past the U.S. border with a fiancé visa. That's pretty good! Skitty tries to climb on the paintings again. "Down! No Skitty!"

"What you say, Kim?"

"No. I'm sorry. I was talking to the cat! Skitty! Down!"

He pauses, "I can't wait to meet your cats." We both smile again over the phone. Omar is coming to New York and will be meeting my two cats. Holy crap.

*   *   *

Today was all-Iraqi all the time!

I met with my *List Project* team to try to help a recently resettled family, as well as plan for the upcoming fundraiser. Then I met with my Iraqi friend Tholfikar. We had dinner and talked about his resettled life here in the U.S. and this girl he likes. And then I went to my Tuesday night Arabic class. Alhamdulillah! The teacher says I am a top student as I make the most mistakes. Wait, what? Apparently, since I am so willing to make loud, public mistakes in class, I am his favorite.

Score. (Or whatever the Arabic equivalent phrase is!)

Somehow, I have a full Iraqi circle in New York. I have unintentionally created a familiar nest for Omar to land in. When he leaves Iraq, it seems I can bring some of Iraq to him.

* * *

"Please, Kim, a question: do people have sex on streets in U.S.?" Omar asks me one day on the phone towards the end of our conversation. I laugh.

"Not usually...but in New York, sure...Why?"

"It just, in yanni, movies, people always having sex in public, on street. Naked. I just wonder if this really happen."

Omar watches so many American movies. He has seen probably more movies than I have. He uses it to learn English and apparently, cultural norms, by Hollywood standards. God help us.

"Not usually, Omar," I smile.

"Oh," he responds, almost disappointed. I feel bad bursting his bubble. I mean, I'm sure someone is having sex on a street somewhere in America. But I find myself wondering: what other messages are we sending to other countries via our movies?

"But maybe you and I can start a new trend," I offer, trying to cheer him up.

"Fuck you," he throws in at me. Well then! I go quiet with this new curse word of his. Did he just tell me to fuck off?

Then, "Is this right use, Kim of 'fuck you'?" he asks. "Is it right how I say it?"

"Yes, more or less." I laugh. "Another movie lesson?"

"Yes! They say it many time in American movies. I like this phrase. 'Fuck you.' This word is funny: fuck. Fuuuck. Fuck you. I like this phrase."

"Fuck you, Omar."

He laughs, "No, fuck you, Kim."

* * *

"You should be president of Iraq," Omar says to me as I'm walking home balancing too many grocery bags and this cursed cell phone. I wasn't expecting him to call. He's been calling a lot more lately. I'm slightly annoyed at the timing but stop for a moment on the corner.

"What? What in the world are you talking about Omar?" I laugh.

The connection is good, but I think he's drunk.

"You should be president of Iraq. Everyone love you. 'Kim so good to us! She sell our painting! We love her,

Omar.' Everyone here say this, they love you Kim." Yup, he's drunk. It seems early in the day to me to be drunk, but then I realize it's midnight in Syria.

"Oh, Omar. You know you're the only one I want to love me." Crap. I didn't mean to say that. I wonder if he understood it. Oh well, he's drunk. I quickly cover with, "Are you drunk, Omar?" My purse slips off my shoulder and I have to adjust all the bags.

"Yes, Kim. I drink Arak tonight. You know I like this drink."

"Yes, I know, Omar. I know how you like that nasty drink!" I laugh. Licorice drinks always skeeve me out. What's the point? One eats licorice. One should not drink it.

"You know I hate that drink, Omar!" I tease.

"Please don't ever hate me Kim," he says. "I need you in my life always."

I pause. "I don't hate you, Omar. Arak. I hate Arak— the drink! Not the country!" I start to walk again, mostly out of discomfort. He is always afraid I will hate him in the end. Whenever *that* will be.

"There should be a statue of you made in Iraq, Kim 'president of Iraq'...oh, and you should be naked in this statue!" He laughs drunkenly.

"Goodbyyyyye, Omar! President of *Arak*! Sleep well!"

"Fuck you!" he teases me with his new favorite English phrase.

I can never walk away from this man, Arak or not, try as I may. But I can hang up. And I do. I wonder if he drinks too much.

President of Iraq...he's crazy. I snicker to myself. Lawwwd, I find him charming.

*   *   *

"No, that box means your mother's maiden name— before she was married. Do you *know* 'maiden name'? Do you have maiden names in Iraq?" Through Omar, I have learned Iraqis have many different name customs than Americans do, and their names are often interchangeable. But the proper usage confuses me. For example, I just learned Omar's real last name today, from his father. What? Why was I using the other name all this time? Iraq is confusing.

"Kim, I not understand." Omar throws out to me, shortness in his voice. This K1 fiancé business overseas, over international connections and over culture is not easy. There's a lot of complicated paperwork and we're both frustrated.

"Can you get someone who speaks better English there to help you, Omar?' I try to delicately ask. "This is just so hard on the phone!"

We are *in* this thing now. We have a lawyer. We have the paperwork. We have the excitement that comes with all this new possibility. What we both need more of now is patience. My lawyer told me this process is slow. It could take between five and twelve months, depending on our luck. So at earliest, that places Omar here in December. Christmas! Wow. Cold *and* Christ. That'll be a shocker for him! Hm. Maybe January is better...

I hope we end up getting married, so I don't screw up his life. I have learned that if we *don't* get married in three months, he has to leave the country or risk being here illegally. So that's something. But neither of us wants to marry for the wrong reasons. Or maybe I do. I don't know. All I know is I love him. But we have both promised honesty at all costs—love *and* marriage or none of the above. So if he comes here and we don't marry, we have a slight challenge on our hands, legally speaking.

"I don't want to live illegal, like Mexican, Kim," he once confided in me when we were discussing potential outcomes. Huh. Even across the globe, people know about our immigration challenges here in the U.S.

"That won't happen, Omar," I try to console. But *I* don't know. It could! He could come all this way and we could learn we hate each other and it was all a fantasy and then what?

"That won't happen, Kim." He always consoles me when I disclose that fear. "We will never hate each other."

My computer has fallen asleep. I take a deep breath, slide the mouse to re-activate the document and continue translating with him.

"Kim, I also want tell you—I learn today there is chance also I could go to Canada on refugee visa. I go to their office and talk to them next week. They say chance is good. They take many Iraqis. Maybe Canada take me."

"Oh, wow," I respond, a little shocked. Competition for my man—from a country this time. "Do you *want* to go to Canada? I mean, I'm confused. What about the fiancé visa to bring you here?"

"I don't know, Kim. I just need something, yes? They said it could be soon. Maybe this is good if fiancé visa does not come. We not know 100% that fiancé come, right?"

"Right. Yeah, I guess you're right. I mean, yes of course, anything to get you out. That's great. I just thought you wanted to come to New York. Do you?"

"Yes, Kim. Of course. But options are good." He actually didn't say the word "options" but he said some other word like it. I was just so filled with an immediate shock and sadness that I don't remember the exact words he said. He might go to Canada instead? What? First universal health care and now Omar!? You're killing me Canada!

"Right, well, you should look into it, I agree. I suppose you should take whichever comes first, right?" I manage to get out. "I mean, I think the important thing is to get you out of Syria."

"Yes, Kim. This is what I think."

"Yes," I agree, half-heartedly. I don't want him in Canada. I want him in New York with me, as selfish as that is. I want the fiancé visa to come first.

"Okay, let's get back to this form!" I say, more eager than ever to finish this paperwork now.

Crap. I hear the stupid phone card woman on the phone line telling me my credit is running low. Crap. Crap. Crap. I forgot to refill it online this morning. I hate this part of things.

"Shoot, Omar. I'm sorry. I'm running out of minutes. We're gonna be disconnected. Finish what you can now and email me what you don't understand, okay Omar?"

She comes on again to warn me of the impending disconnection. "Okay, did you understand me, O—"

Three Visas

And he's gone. Or I am. Dead air. I put down my phone and close my computer and lean back. Please let the fiancé visa comes first.

*   *   *

I still don't know Omar's "story". Isn't that funny? I have no idea why he initially left Baghdad, what horrors befell him. I often wonder why that has never come up in our twelve thousand conversations, both virtual and otherwise. Maybe he has no interest in remembering it. Maybe I am too afraid to ask. Maybe I am still too full of stories. Maybe it doesn't even matter anymore. Maybe we're creating a new story.

*   *   *

I'm on a ranch in North Dakota with my mom, my sister and her family, enjoying a bit of pastoral scenery while visiting extended relatives. I am leaning on a corral fence and in front of me are horses and sky. This is pure movie. Doesn't seem real.

I snuck away to call Omar. I miss him. It's been about a month since we mailed in the K1 papers. We are now just waiting; he in Damascus and I in North Dakota. Somehow I got myself further from Omar. Maybe that's why I miss him so much.

I can't stop thinking of him up here. I wish he were here. I want him here. He would love it, I know.

"Describe it more, Kim. Is it green?" Omar asks, hungry for more details of North Dakota.

"Yes, it's very lush."

"What is lush?"

"Um. Green. And thick. It's very green and hilly and wide open. North Dakota is wide open."

"Is it like cowboy movies?"

"Yes, I suppose it is." I chuckle. Omar and his movie references...

"Let's ride horses someday, Kim. Habibti, you want this?" Our phone calls have been so flirty and romantic again lately. It makes me happy, hopeful.

"Yes, sounds great! I would love that, Omar," I respond. It's always charming to me—the things he wants to do that he never has—horseback riding, bike riding, eating pork. I too, want to do them all with him. I want to share in those firsts with him. The thought of it makes me giddy—sharing all his discoveries. And his bacon.

"It's lovely, really. I love it here. You would love all the green."

"Yes, I can't wait to see what green looks like on the Earth." Again. Firsts. Seeing green. I want to be with him when he sees green. God, I'm in love with this man. I want to be with him when he sees green.

"It's quiet, relaxing, wide open. So much space. It's like the opposite of New York City."

"Yes, yes. I imagine, Kim. Someday, I would like to live in a place like this."

"Really? You want to live in North Dakota?" I laugh.

"Sure, Kim. Someday, I would like to live on, yanni— how you call it…a farm? Yes, a farm and have some animals, not too many. Just a few. And water and trees. I want a garden and I would go for a walk every day and come home to my wife. I would paint in the afternoons, after taking …you know, yanni, my favorite word you teach me—"

"A nap?" I offer smiling, listening to this idyllic life he is describing.

"Yes, Kim. A nap! I would come home and take a nap. I would like this life. Very much." He pauses. "Do you think it stupid?"

I smile. "Not at all, Omar." I want to play the part of the "wife". "I would like this life too. Maybe I'm ready to get out of New York. I don't know. What you described sounds perfect."

"Really, Kim? Really?"

I would be ready for any life with him—North Dakota
or not! A horse whinnies in the nearby coral, and a manure-
infused breeze blows by. I take a deep breath. Yup. Any
life at all.

*   *   *

IM Aug 5, 2011

`03:09:48` PM `k:` oh hey! Happy Eid! Eid Mubarek!

[AUTHOR'S NOTE: Muslim Day]

`03:10:06` PM `o:` thank u kim so much

`03:10:11` PM `k:` your welcome.

`03:10:13` PM `k:` it's today yes? The holiday?

`03:10:13` PM `o:` yes and to u

`03:10:18` PM `k:` why thank you!

`03:10:24` PM `k:` I'm almost more Muslim than you

`03:10:38` PM `k:` right?

`03:10:39` PM `o:` u r ☺

IM Sep 13, 2011

`11:09:35` AM `k:` omar. I need to ask you.

`11:09:44` AM `k:` Are you sure you want the fiancé visa instead of
just waiting for the refugee visa with Canada?

`11:10:03` AM `o:` yes kim but if my case with Canada sacseed in a
short time

`11:10:29` AM `o:` i will do it - may be with u it still take a long time
right?

```
11:11:10 AM o: u understand?

11:12:04 AM k: i do... And I want to get you out of Syria but...

11:12:20 AM o: what

11:12:28 AM k: it worries me

11:12:45 AM o: yes

11:13:05 AM k: At some point though...I think you will have to
               commit to doing the fiancé visa with me

11:13:29 AM k: the government will be involved

11:14:03 AM o: wait kim

11:14:11 AM o: dictsonary

11:15:26 AM k: This is what I meant Omar, when I asked "are we
               doing this?"

11:15:46 AM k: But I know you have to make something work....

11:16:06 AM k: so I guess we will just keep moving forward on
               both fronts and see

11:16:22 AM k: it's just you know there is a lawyer working for us
               and she is now involved

11:16:29 AM k: It's not just you and I.

11:16:56 AM k: this paperwork will be filed and at a certain point,
               there's no turning back.

11:16:56 AM k: and it just makes me a little scared--legally

11:17:08 AM k: do you understand any of that?

11:18:19 AM o: look kim

11:18:25 AM o: i trust in u

11:18:41 AM o: till me what shold i do

11:19:12 AM o: and i will do it
```

11:19:43 AM k: You need to think hard about whether you want a life in canada or whether you want to come to NY and live with me.

11:19:51 AM k: because both seem possible right now

11:20:06 AM o: new york with you

*   *   *

"I promise not to cry this time. Just tell me what you need to say, Omar." He asked to talk to me today, said it was important. I'm curled up on the infamous orange chair ready for what's next, always what's next. Will this ever end?

"I know myself, Kim. If I come New York, I can't stay long time with you. With anyone, I mean. You know? I am independent. Many years independent."

"Okay," I respond, dipping my feet in the waters of this conversation. "I mean, I assumed you would live with me for a while at least. I mean where else would you go?" What is happening right now?

"Yes, I just want space."

What did he just say? "I haven't seen you for almost three years and I need *space*?"

"No, Kim. Please. I'm sorry. In the first, I need you. Yes. And will live with you. Maybe always live with you. I don't know. We don't know yet, right? I just don't want make you tired and I want you be comfortable. Don't want to make you worry. Understand me or not, Kim?"

I sit there a minute thinking. I feel hurt. Should I be? He's being honest, what I have always asked of him. But it sounds like he's already planning his escape from me.

"Habibti?"

"I just..." I almost stop but push through. Some police sirens go screaming by my window. "I knew what it meant when I offered you the fiancé visa, Omar. I was willing to do this. I mean, I want to help you. But ultimately, I also want an answer to the age-old Omar question in my life."

"What, Kim? Wait. Dictionary."

"No, Omar. You don't need the dictionary. Just listen to me." I take in a big breath. "Don't you also want an answer to the Kim question? Whether this is something? Whether this relationship is real?"

The sirens are quiet. So is Omar. I'm not sure if the answer is no or if he doesn't understand the question.

"I feel like you are always running from me, Omar," I bravely say.

"Kim, please don't."

"Don't what? Tell you how I feel? If the answer to the Omar or Kim question is no, then fine. So be it. There's our answer. Our ending. Finally, but it's a lot harder for *you* if we don't fall in love and get married."

"What is that mean?"

"I'm sorry. I just mean asylum will be hard. You should know that. And if we don't marry, you'll have to apply for asylum. I mean, it can happen. But it will be easier if we fall in love."

*   *   *

IM Dec 8, 2011

12:42:59 PM o: kim

12:43:06 PM o: i want ask u cwasthin

12:43:19 PM k: question

12:43:21 PM o: qwastion

12:43:24 PM k: question ☺

12:43:25 PM o: yes question ☺

12:43:38 PM o: i mean since we have no fiance visa

12:43:45 PM o: if i can go to vancouver

12:43:56 PM o: maybe in febreary on refugee visa instead

12:44:40 PM k: I'm listening

12:44:15 PM o: its near to u s yes?

12:45:46 PM o: what u think? we can still see each other

12:45:51 PM k: well yes, but...it's harder

12:46:00 PM k: I had hoped the K1 visa would be here by now too. It's already December

12:45:58 PM o: its near to u -canada?

12:46:06 PM k: sort of... yes...

Three Visas

12:46:54 PM k: we should hear something on K1 visa this month or January at latest I think

12:47:03 PM k: I hope

12:47:54 PM k: I think it's an important decision for you

12:48:21 PM k: K1 does some things for you and us but refugee visa is safer and will pay for airline ticket from Syria

12:48:37 PM k: I think we always said whichever comes first, yes?

12:48:22 PM o: but u know i should not lose any chance or

12:48:55 PM o: salution

12:49:02 PM k: yes

12:49:14 PM o: becose you know what may be happen here

12:49:24 PM o: maybe soon it be like Iraq here

12:49:38 PM o: and u want me be safe

12:49:43 PM k: yes of course

12:49:49 PM k: I want you out of there as soon as possible too

12:50:16 PM k: let's talk about this on the phone later omar

12:50:28 PM o: y u sad?

12:50:36 PM k: ahh omar

12:50:42 PM k: I'm not sad....

12:50:44 PM o: what

12:50:45 PM k: ok, maybe a little

12:50:45 PM o: kimy y?

12:50:50 PM k: Why do u think? Of course, I want what's best for you

12:50:58 PM o: i know

12:51:03 PM k: but selfishly I want you here

12:51:40 PM o: Oh habibti

IM Dec 20, 2011

11:57:55 AM k: Isn't it funny how much I can miss you after not seeing you for 2 years?

IM Dec 25, 2011

06:36:26 PM k: Merry Christmas Omar

10:51:14 PM o: Merry Christmas Kim think of you.

IM Jan 7, 2012

01:16:34 PM o: hi kim I just want till you that we should not talk every day on foon it's not good for me

01:18:37 PM o: you know we dont want problem with .... you know

01:18:57 PM o: i want to stay safe to go to you

IM Jan 17, 2012

02:03:57 PM o: kim stop everything

02:19:00 PM o: im wory stop eveyrthing

09:43:36 PM k: omar. What's going on? I got your messages. Stop what? Are you ok?

*   *   *

I am almost hysterical as commuters rush past me to get into the train station on 96th street. I am blocking the entrance. I don't care. Go around me.

"Please, Omar. Explain what is going on. *Why* can't I call you? Please!" I am pacing now in front of the train entrance, making it even trickier for the commuters to enter. I was standing at the top of the stairs just about to descend to the train when my phone rang.

"What are you afraid of, Omar?"

"Kim, I hear stories. This is Syria. You know this. People disappear. Iraqis disappear. This is not safe for us to talk so much. They listen. The government." He whispers that last part. "I am worried is all."

"Oh my God, Omar." I never imagined my life like this. I am out of my element, still. I never imagined I would be in love with a man in a foreign country who couldn't talk to me for fear of death. This isn't what happens in America. I don't know how to process all this. It's all so different and overwhelming to me that I start to cry. More hurried rush hour commuters annoyingly push past the crying girl blocking the stairs. I stand to the side at last. There is a chill in the late afternoon air. I am late for drinks with a friend. And I'm so, so tired.

Is this for real or is he just being paranoid? I can't tell. Would he be arrested, deported or even killed for repeated calls with an American? I mean, really? Maybe this is just a trick to get me to call him less. Am I calling him too much? No, that's ridiculous. Syria is falling apart. There is genuine danger and he is genuinely scared. We are so close to getting him out of there. Please God: help him last a little longer. Help *me* last a little longer. Keep him safe. I couldn't handle it if something happened to him—not now. Not after all this.

"Okay, Omar," I offer. "I won't call. I'll wait for you to IM me then, when you can."

"Yes, Kim. I think this is best."

"Please be careful, Omar. I'm scared." He says nothing. I need him to say something, to reassure me, but he is incapable right now of doing such a thing. Not knowing what else to say, I offer, "I'm so sorry you have to live like this. But soon you will be out."

"Insha'Allah, Kim. Insha'Allah."

Insha'Allah. I click off my phone and stand in the middle of the sidewalk, exhausted, allowing myself to get lost for a minute in the busy New York City life swirling and spinning around me. I imagine Omar standing in his street doing the same thing in Damascus. We're so far away.

*   *   *

The moon is out again tonight. It's almost full. As I walk home from the train, I look up and I wonder if Omar is looking at the moon right now too. Since New York hides its stars in all the bright lights, the moon plays a good stand in. I like that we share the same moon—somehow that makes me feel better. I exhale. And dream.

*   *   *

Western Union just called me. I think. I was sitting at my computer working when a blocked number came through.

"Kim Schultz, please."

"Speaking."

"Ms. Schultz, this is Western Union. Sorry to bother you but we wanted to ask you a few questions," a very friendly female voice says. I stand up and start to walk toward my window of cell reception.

"Yes?" I respond with equal parts suspicion and impatience. What could Western Union want? I haven't sent money to Omar for paintings for a couple of months now. What issues with payment could there be?

"We have noticed you have sent money several times to Syria and Iraq. Is that true?"

"Yes. Is there a problem?"

"No problem. May I ask why you sent this money?"

I hesitate. What did she just ask me? "You may not," I somehow remarkably manage to say. I could tell her I help sell Iraqi refugee's art. That's where the money comes from, but I don't want trouble, if trouble is to be had. And what business can it be of hers?

"Fine. We just wanted to be sure you are ok."

Wait, what? "What do you mean? What?" I ask.

"We want to be sure you are not doing something…against your will," she replies awkwardly.

"No, I'm fine. Why are you asking me this?"

"Well with repeated large amount sent to certain countries, we want to make sure the person isn't being…taken advantage of. Can you tell me why you are sending money to these countries?"

"No, I cannot," I said. "It's none of your business." I was starting to get mad now. First of all, it's not "large" amounts of money. It's in the hundreds. Secondly, she has already asked me that. What is going on? Something is off.

"I understand. Well, thank you so much for your time. We're glad everything is in order. Have a wonderful day." And she was gone. Hung up. I sit looking at my phone, dumbfounded. Why did Western Union just call me? *Did* Western Union just call me? Oh my God, was that the government? And whose government?

What's happening in my life right now?

* * *

Well, at least the pasta is good. As is often the case, Randy and I are sitting at one of our fave Italian places on the upper west side of Manhattan. And he's dishin' out more than Bolognese.

"I think it's time to walk away. All he does is causes you heartache. You know this! It's been so long, Kim—so long!"

"I know, I know," I respond. I know he's right. This is all too hard and complicated. And after almost three years of listening to this saga unfold, Randy is justifiably frustrated. I look out the window at the flurries that are starting and regret not wearing my boots. The first clean snow in New York is always so lovely. It's one of my favorite things. Omar should have been here for it. He should have been here by now.

Randy drags me back into the restaurant with his words. "I wanted the happy ending as much as you did, Kim. Honest! I wanted it for you, but I mean—come on! Enough is enough."

"I know," I repeat, unable to think of anything new to say. And then of course Donna Summer's classic, *Enough Is Enough* starts playing in my head.

"He disappears. He makes you cry. Maybe its just time to end it." *It's raining (raining), pouring (pouring).*

"How do I end it, Randy? I mean, we have a fiancé visa! I'm waiting to hear from the stupid U.S. government if he can come here and I can have a chance at this! How do I end it now? I'm in too deep." I start to cry now. Again. In a restaurant. "I have to see it through. I want to see it through. What else can I do?"

I wipe my tears and sip my merlot. *My love life is boring me to tears—after all theeeese years...*

"Fine," he relents. "So we wait for the visa to come or not and then we'll reassess." Randy's use of business terms for my deeply personal turmoil always makes me smile. I relax a little. Yes, we'll reassess.

"Omar and I always agreed that we would take whichever visa comes first—Canada or the K1. So fate, or the government, will decide it. We just need to get him out of there," I sigh.

"Ok, I just don't want to keep seeing you get hurt." I know, I know—my mom, Catherine, everyone feels the same way.

And we won't waste another...tear. (Let's be honest: we probably will)

I push my plate away. I've had enough–of it all. It's so hard to believe enough for everyone.

*   *   *

"Omar? It's me. I'm sorry, did I wake you?" That question is ridiculous. I know I did. It's after 3 a.m. in Damascus, but I had to call. It's been a couple of weeks since our last phone call and I just got home after a long day. I did as he asked and initiated no communication. But now, my mail is scattered on the counter and I am frozen, holding one particular letter in my hand, almost shaking, not believing the words I see, after all this time.

"Yes Kim, but it ok. What is it? Are you all right?" he said in his not-very-clear-just-woke-up English.

"Yes, yes. I just got home and got my mail and guess what?" My heart was palpitating in my throat, as I held the letter in my hands. "We got the K1 visa. We got approved for the fiancé visa, Omar!" I laugh.

There is silence. "Omar, do you understand?" I excitedly ask. Maybe the line was cut again.

"Kim, I am sleeping. I don't understand everything you say. Can you call tomorrow?"

I pause. One of my cats comes up to me and rubs herself against my leg. She must be prophetic with her comfort. We just learned we got approved to get Omar out of the mess of Syria and into my arms after waiting six months…and he wants me to call him tomorrow? Skitty meows gently. I want to scream loudly.

"Omar, do you understand what I'm saying?" I unintentionally slide down my kitchen wall to the floor, all the chairs evidently too far away.

"No Kim, please, but I am sleeping. I drink very much tonight. I sorry. Can we tomorrow talk? You can tell me all then, ok?"

Are you kidding me?

"You don't want to wake up and talk about this? We got the visa!" I quickly blurt out. He doesn't want to wake up from his drunken stupor and talk about the fact I just got the goddamn visa?

"Kim. I not understand you. I so tired. You're talking fast. Please. Can we just talk tomorrow?"

"Fine. Goodnight," I reply, angry, shocked, heartbroken. I know he was sleeping, but *this* is the moment. This is the moment we have been waiting for, or I have been waiting for. I got the U.S. government to issue him a visa! I did! Omar can come to New York! He can live with me. We can see if this relationship is real and can last. This is our shot. My shot? Our shot. And he's too tired to wake himself up to understand the impact of this news. Am I the only one excited that I just got him out of Syria? Is he even *in* this relationship with me? I sit on the floor trying to assess how bad this is. Reassess. Is this bad? Is it a sign of his commitment (or lack thereof) to me or am I overreacting?

I re-read the letter from the Department of Homeland Security with the official U.S. seal once again: *Approval notice, I129F Petition for Fiancé. The above petition has been approved.*

The United States government believes we are in love. Why doesn't he?

*   *   *

IM Feb 25, 2012

11:37:29 PM o: Kim I think it is best if I wait for visa with Canada
I am sorry I think it best.

11:37:37 PM o: Please understand

... is what Omar IM-ed me a few minutes ago. He's choosing Canada. We always said we would take whatever visa came first, whatever would get him out of Syria first. But now, when presented with the fiancé visa on a silver platter, he is choosing Canada. I don't get it. We have the K1 visa. It came first! I won! But now he doesn't seem to want it. Me.

Clearly we need to talk. But it's on him this time. I'm done initiating. I'm done calling. I'm done fighting. I'm done. Period.

Three Days in Damascus

He can come to me.

* * *

I remember going to a house in Syria. The wife and daughter offered us tea as usual. We said "yes" as usual and proceeded to talk with the father about their situation, as usual. It was the middle of the day and I didn't give anything a second thought really, but something nudged me to go into the kitchen with the women. I found a moment to excuse myself and did just that.

In the kitchen I found the women working in the dark. I hadn't noticed because of the daylight, but apparently there was no electricity here either. And instead of not offering us tea, they built a small "campfire" in the kitchen—an actual live fire on the countertop on which they were taking turns holding the hot teapot with their bare hands over the lapping flames until the water boiled. They were doing this for me out of custom, out of hospitality, out of generosity. I was so moved by this act, but it would never have dawned on them to do otherwise. There were going to serve their guests regardless of their situation. They looked over their shoulders at me. I smiled softly and returned to the main room.

Tradition and culture are strong. Nothing ever really stops them, does it?

Three Visas

*   *   *

Turns out Omar has agreed to an arranged marriage with
an Iraqi—a Muslim—Arab woman. Everything I am not—
well, except the woman part. Yup, you read that right.
There it is. There's the missing piece. He finally came to
me and there's the explanation. After three years, I fell for
a man who instead of marrying me, agreed to marry a
woman he doesn't know or love, just because she is Iraqi
and his family asked him too. Unbelievable. He tells me
this has been in the works for a while now, but he finally
agreed to it last week, right before the fiancé visa came
through.

Are you kidding me? He's known about this for weeks
and only telling me now?

"My parents are set in their ways. They think this is
best for me, Kim. I am thirty-nine years. This is very old in
my world," Omar pleaded into my cell phone.

Old in *your* world? Try being forty, single and living
in New York City! Sorry, I digress.

I am listening to this late-breaking, life-changing news
on my cell phone while riding the Bolt Bus to Boston (the
first failed title of this book). On the 'Bolt Bus to Boston',
on my way to do the play again, the damn, damned love
story again—is where I am when Omar drops this

235

bombshell of information: arranged marriage, while he has another offered marriage waiting for him in the U.S.A. Well, that's a game changer. And here I am on the Bolt Bus in a public pile of interstate tears.

"What, Omar? What?" I maybe oh-so-succinctly ask. I'm not entirely sure. I am shell-shocked. Bomb-shell shocked. Suicide-bomber-bomb-shell-shocked. My bus mates even feel the reverberations. They look at me. So much of this relationship has been in public, why should the breakup be any different? Are "other" people listening to us? Is "Western Union" spying on me right now? I don't care. Bring it!

Omar keeps talking, but my mind is spinning, swirling, swimming.

"They think I'm gay or broken, or something wrong with me," he continues, "They want me married! You know, it is hard to change the mind of the Orientals."

Arranged marriage, arranged marriage. Did he just say Oriental? I'm not allowed to say that word. Arranged marriage? Arranged marriage? Spin. Swirl. Swim. Shit.

"Are you kidding me right now, Omar? Are you fucking *kidding* me?" I even more succinctly ask. Strangers on the Bolt Bus steal more glances at me, worried about the "crazy" that is developing in their close quarters. I try to turn into the window to hide my tears. Funny, hiding my tears just like on that bus in Lebanon, unable to stop crying. I have come full circle. I rest my forehead against the glass, wishing for anything but this.

"Kim, please. What choice I have?" he pleads, thousands of miles and hundreds of centuries away.

"You could marry me," I want to say, my voice dripping with sarcasm. "I thought you might marry *me!*" But I don't know if I say that out loud or not. I don't know what I said. *This* is why he's been so quiet. *This* is why he thinks Canada is better for him. *This* is why. He's marrying some else. Oh my God. He's marrying someone else.

*   *   *

There was a story I heard when I was in Jordan or Lebanon, I can't remember which, about a married couple that awoke in their home in Baghdad one night to a horrifically loud noise. They opened their eyes to see a rocket glide between them onto the bed. A rocket! It had somehow not detonated, but nonetheless crashed through the walls of their home, slowly gliding right between them on the bed, pausing. At first, they both lay there looking at this rocket in their bed, and then ever so slowly they got out of bed and fled the house. Both of them were fine. An undetonated rocket. In their bed. Lying between them.

Mine detonated.

*   *   *

On the phone, a day after the Bolt Bus debacle, we are both still crying. I am in Boston sitting on the floor against my bed, trying to process what just happened and assess what can be salvaged from the rubble. He keeps calling to talk and I keep picking up, despite that fact that tonight I need to perform our "love story" under these new and exciting circumstances. Apparently, he is in Damascus dithering in uncertainty as to whether he made the right choice or not in choosing her. Are you *kidding* me? *Now* you're weighing options? You do that *before* you destroy my life, not after, idiot.

In the last twenty-four hours, I have tried to resign myself to this new fate, his supposed fate, now my own, mostly just to assure myself I can get through the play in one piece.

"Just tell me you're happy, Omar." I offer as a peace token, honestly hoping he's not.

Pregnant pause.

"I'm *not* happy, Kim. I think I made mistake," Omar confesses.

Huh. Well, there's a doozy. Not the answer I expected. What do I say to that? "Good! You made your bed, now lie in it?" That's mean, plus he'd never understand it. He's barely fluent, let alone proficient in idioms.

"Why then, Omar? Why did you do this?" I was starting to get mad at him again, always creating these windows of hope for me where I wish he would for once build a brick wall.

"My family, Kim. They want this. They want me married to an Iraqi girl before I leave Middle East. This is important to them, Kim. This is our culture. You know this."

"What about me? Why won't you fight for a chance for us, Omar? Don't you want to fight for us? I got us the visa! All I ever wanted was a chance!"

"Kim, please. This is so hard. Please. What choice I have?"

At that point, I could do or ask no more. The walls came tumbling down. I just lay down the phone and my body on the floor, swearing off any further contact with Omar for some time at least, wondering how I allowed myself to fall this hard and this long for this Iraqi man; wondering how I get home from here.

Three Days in Damascus

Three Months in Mexico

Today, ten months after we were approved for the wasted fiancé visa and three months since we've spoken, I learned, through *Facebook*, (apropos for a relationship conducted primarily through technology) that Omar is in Canada—resettled at last—in Canada. Alone, sans fiancé. But he made it.

O.M.Y.

Oh Canada! — As the anthem goes, giving refuge to my refugee.

And here I sit in Mexico: palm trees, cool breeze, white sands, coral reef, Mexico. I came here a month ago to write, breathe and be near water and air and sky. I can't seem to leave. It wasn't initially, intentionally about avoiding Omar, although maybe on some level it was. I needed space, more space than the distance between New York and Vancouver could provide. It's as if once I knew he was coming to my continent, I needed to flee to the other end of it. Apparently we have a self-imposed 6,000-mile-minimum-between-us rule. Ridiculous. But I needed that distance, I guess. I needed to take some control in a situation continually and wildly out of my control. As Donna Summer and myself in a NYC restaurant once sang, "Enough is enough."

At least at last he is safe, resettled. For that I am grateful. His fiancé is still refugee-ing in Cairo. Who knows what will happen there. Nothing ever seems definite, but I'm done waiting for him to make a choice. I'm making my own.

And now the real work of resettlement for him begins. All he knows, changes. Life begins again. With all the work I have done these past three years with resettled refugees, I know his work is only now beginning, as I am searching for the end. We are ironically both, it seems, simultaneously resettled *and* unsettled.

Here in Mexico, I have been able to find my distance from Omar that I was never able to find in New York. Here I finally don't call or text or IM daily. And nor does he. We are letting each other breathe. Here I am starting to gain perspective on this foray into love, culture and war. Here I write *this* story. And here I no longer cry over him—except for tonight, the night I learn he is finally safe in Canada.

Sitting on the empty beach, sand in my toes, eyes on the sea, waves pounding my heart—tonight, I cry. I cry an ocean of tears. With our shared moon starting to climb the sky, I cry for what could have been, for what I thought was. I cry because I am not with Omar in Canada right now. I cry because he is alone. I cry because I am too. I cry for what has been lost, never to be found. I cry for what is broken. And I cry for *all* the Iraqis broken, still trapped in dangerous lands, not their own. I cry for all those who have already died by the hands of this invasion. I cry for those who have no family and no future, no hope, no dreams. I cry for what we have done and for what we have left undone. I cry: oh, *Omar, Omar, Omar.* I cry.

I look up and see the most beautiful bed of stars almost dancing in the night sky.

Nejoom.

Three Days in Damascus

Three Days in Vancouver

"Tell my whole story so that the world may know."

"I can't believe I am finally seeing Omar," I texted to the man himself yesterday in an odd third-person way. "I can't wait to see Kim too," Omar responded in third-person just as playfully. And with neither English, nor commitment his strong suit, he added, "But only us know that."

Except for his best friend Alaa, he told no one I was coming to Vancouver to see him, not his family and certainly not his Iraqi fiancé still living in Cairo. I'm not sure how I feel about this, our secret liaison. Because I, on the other hand, told *everyone* I was *finally* seeing the elusive Omar again. After all, it's my dream come true. He says he doesn't want to tell her because he doesn't want to hurt her. Well neither do I! I don't want to hurt an innocent caught in the crosshairs. Arranged or otherwise.

"I wish you would tell her, Omar," I texted him before I bought the ticket. "Just tell her we need to see each other, after all these years."

"She would not understand, Kim," he replied.

I'm not even certain I understand. I wonder if I should even be going. He's still engaged, after all. Whether he ends up married or not, he's still engaged and I know the score. (Kim: 0) But I also know I need to see him. I need an answer. I need my ending. And this need to see him outweighs *everything* else. Honestly, I see no choice in the matter. And so, against the advice of most of my family, friends and my own better judgment, I decided I would still go. I simply couldn't live with the regret of never knowing. Thus with very little conversation or planning, I simply bought a one-way ticket to Vancouver. I would see Omar and I would figure out later how to return home. Ironic. And through our now common communication method, I texted Omar about my plans to visit.

"Good Kim! I await you!" was his response. Well then. That's that. Good! He awaits me.

I'm thinking about this as I await Omar in the ugly lobby of the apartment building I'm staying at in Vancouver. I decided against staying at his place (too tempting!), a hotel (too expensive!) and his best friend Alaa's house (too scandalous!) and landed on an apartment rental that I thought would be best. Turns out, it's kinda scary...and smoky—cheap, scary and smoky. Oh well. Omar is here. Omar is on his way to see me. Nothing else really matters in my mind.

I am trying to keep my cool, but I am visibly shaking. I am so nervous and so happy all at once. I stand looking at myself in the lobby mirror. Here I am. This is who is going to see Omar. This woman. This Kim. After all this time, Omar, *my* Omar, is on his way to me. After all these years, tonight, I see Omar again. Holy crapoly.

I step outside. Man, it's freezing out. I don't think I dressed warm enough for this cold. I wanted to look cute, but not too cute. I wanted to show cleavage, but not too much cleavage. You know what I mean. So I shiver. Women are stupid around men. I should have dressed warmer.

Where is he? Of course he's late. Of course Omar, my Arab poster boy, is late! I laugh and sit on a bench. I am now choosing to find it amusing. It's a new me!

I see a man walk up the snowy sidewalk, head hanging down. Is that Omar? OMY. Is it? I wait a few more steps before I stand up. It's him. I can see him now. I inhale, trying to remember to breathe. He sees me, pauses and then starts to laugh. I can see him laughing. I start to laugh. He keeps walking toward me as my eyes well up. Damn me and my incessant tears. And as he gets close enough to touch, we instinctually throw our arms around one another.

"Is it you?" He asks or I ask, I don't remember who said what anymore. These first moments are a blur—a hazy, intoxicating blur.

"Habibti," he says. Oh! Please not *that* word! It's not fair. It's the one word I love the most. It will push me over the edge! Omar, Omar, Omar. I am trying not to cry, but failing. I see he is too. How similar we both are. He shivers and we hold each other crying, freezing.

"Oh, Omar," I say, as he kisses me. We hug again. We kiss again. We kiss and hug some more, neither of us certain what to do now—the surrealism exceeding the reality.

Finally: Omar. Finally.

And now what?

"Kimmy," he says, and we laugh. We stand there on the empty sidewalk in a snowy Vancouver neighborhood simply looking at each other, laughing. It's been three years and even more tears. He kisses me again, takes my hands and says, "I don't know what to do. Should we walk?"

So not knowing what else to do, we walk, looking at each other, holding hands. So much has happened since we saw each other last—a revolution, a resettlement...an engagement. I work very hard to keep myself present. I try to breathe, but I feel like I am out of my body or in someone else's. I'm back to that hazy, intoxicating blur again. He is talking, but about what I cannot tell you. I don't remember how to listen. I don't remember how to speak. I barely remember how to walk, but every so often, I laugh.

"What?" he finally asks, after one of my random outbursts of laughter.

"I just can't believe you're talking." I respond. It sounds stupid, but it's what I felt. Omar is talking to me, in person—Omar!

"I don't know what I say, Kim. I have no idea what I talk about. I just talk because I don't know what else to do." We both laugh. Me too, Omar.

"I want kiss you." He declares. I stop and look at him, then smile and shake my head.

"We're not sleeping together," I reply. He squeezes my hand tighter, laughs and we keep walking, as I lean into him, smiling.

"You said you were going to save Iraq. Why do you not?"

We find a bar—not an easy task in this crappy neighborhood. In front of me is a beer and Omar. Crazy. I like them both.

We settle in, making odd small talk. But in under an hour, it's already all coming out. Not about his fiancé. I can't talk about her yet. Too soon. But everything else is game after three years of waiting for answers. My questions are like bullets.

And after a few, Omar answers, "Kim, please, I don't know, ok?"

"That's not enough Omar. You *texted* me that you fell in love with another woman. How could you do that? Didn't you know that would kill me?" He is looking down at his whiskey, avoiding me.

"Omar, please. I've waited years to talk to you about these things. I deserve an answer. I need to know if I was crazy or if this was *ever* real to you." I am crying. You'd think the well would be dry by now. "Why did you tell me like that?"

"I don't know, Kim. It was so long ago. Things were not real. I was so scared. I didn't know what to do. I thought you would be happy for me. I'm sorry. I not know, Kim."

He thought I would be happy. What was he thinking? I could never be happy when the man I fell in love with fell in love with another woman—not then or now.

"I was confused. I sorry Kim. We are friends. I never want to make you cry."

Well, for a man who never wants to make me cry, he sure does make me cry! I exhale and look at him. I have to ask it in person.

"Do you love her?"

"Shadiya?" he asks, summoning the name we do not speak. I nod. He pauses. I wait. Finally, he confesses, "She loves me. She is a kind girl. I think I will grow to love her."

Then neither of us says anything, living in this new reality.

"Let's get out of here," I quickly say, incapable of having this conversation yet. "Show me Vancouver!"

"There is no place called home now."

Lying in bed the next morning, I roll over and look at Omar. Well, crap—here we are again.

"This is not my life. This is zero."

The crosswalk light changes and Omar grabs my hand to cross the street. I love that he does that. He does it every time we cross a street. He's a gentleman. If we're not already holding hands, he grabs mine and off we go. Safety first! It reminds me of when we held hands in Damascus; except there, of course, it was dangerous. Here in Canada? Not so much. I think it's gallant.

We cross the intersection and he places my arm at his elbow. It's cold. I snuggle in. I find my crook again, upright this time. I like being taken care of. I like Omar. I wish I didn't. I wish I had been wrong about us. I wish it would have turned out that we were a mismatch, that we didn't get along this well, that somehow I was wrong about us. But I wasn't. We're everything I thought we were. In person, our relationship is exactly as I imagined it all these years online—except for the unexpected and unnecessary fiancé between us.

Several people pass by us on the street talking loudly. It pulls me out of my reverie. I catch Omar looking at me. I look up at him and smile. I don't want this to ever end.

It's funny. I start to think. What if I made it to Damascus? What if we had seen each other again sooner? Would things have turned out differently? Maybe he wouldn't have agreed to an arranged marriage. Maybe he would have stood up to his family. Maybe things would have been different. Maybe.

Suddenly aware of our location, I look around us and announce, "Omar, I think we're going the wrong way. I think the train is this way." We are heading in the opposite direction we want. I am certain of it. I start to pull him in the direction I think it is. Or rather, that I *know* it is. Vancouver is a pretty easy city to get around in. But I try not to make it too obvious, so as not to offend him. This is *his* city, after all. But he continues walking in the same direction.

"Omar, seriously!" I laugh as I say it, but it's really cold and I'm not in the mood to walk unnecessarily out of our way in this weather, strong Arab male ego present or not.

"Kim," Omar, half-laughing, half-serious, teases, "Why can't you just do what I say and be more like..." He stops himself.

My jaw drops, "...like an Arab girl?" I finish for him. "Be more like an Arab girl and do as you say? Is that what you meant?"

We have stopped in the middle of an intersection and I look at him at this literal and metaphorical crossroads, neither of us moving for a moment, suddenly face to face with our cultures, until I break the tension and smile. "Don't worry, Omar. You're *marrying* a nice Arab girl, a nice Iraqi girl, who will likely do exactly what you tell her." That one cut a little too close to the bone for both of us and the smile on both our faces fades, as we feel the impact of what I just said: He's marrying an Iraqi woman, not me. There. I said it. It's out.

We walk almost a block in silence, at which point Omar finally realizes we are walking in the wrong direction. He stops and looks at me.

"Kim. Why you not tell me we walk in the wrong direction? You really should speak up more. Be more..." he pauses, smiling, waiting for me to finish it.

"American? Fuck you." We both laugh as he grabs my hand and we head back in the direction we came from. Although I suspect we would have managed, inside my head, I comfort myself by thinking: it would have been a damn long bumpy road.

"Look! Look in our cupboards! Empty! We have nothing!"

"Please sit," Omar says, gesturing to the one recently vacated train seat.

"No, thanks," I respond. Although my feet are sore from walking, I would rather stand here next to him, holding his hand. I am treasuring every borrowed moment. We look at each other and smile. I still can't believe I'm here with Omar. Twenty-four hours later and it still startles me that we are here together.

His fiancé has been calling quite a bit. It makes us both feel uncomfortable and guilty. Neither of us likes it, but this is the bed we made—literally. I convince myself it's ok, that we deserve this. We deserve a shot. Their long-distance shotgun engagement took away my shot at love and I deserve a shot—*we* deserve a shot before he decides to marry her. I just doubt she would see things the same way. The train lurches from the station.

"So, I'll just go to my place and you to yours and we'll meet again in two hours, yes? And we'll have a lovely New Year's Eve dinner," I say to Omar, confirming our previously discussed plans. This will be the first time we have been apart since being together, but he has to call Shadiya and I have to give him space. I already miss him, even though he's not mine to miss.

"Yes, Kim, two hours." The train begins to slow again. "Kim, this next stop is yours, please." I squeeze his hand. He smiles in response. This is complicated and layered and certainly not easy, but so far worth it. I am with Omar and it is delicious. The train doors open.

"This is you. Go, Kim, hurry!" he tries to push me out. Relax, I think. I live in New York. I know trains. I have *loads* of time before the doors close, so I go back for a quick last-minute kiss.

"Kim, the doors!" Omar laughs, as we hurriedly kiss goodbye. We could never do this in Syria. I want him to know it's okay to kiss in public here.

"Okay! See you soon, Omar!" I shout, as the doors almost close on me before I'm out.

Huh. Trains make quicker stops here than in New York City. Note to self.

I wave at him as his train pulls out. I almost *skip* I'm so happy. This is what I wanted. Ping the rest.

"I want to feel human again."

Another text comes in from Omar. But like the previous two, I ignore it. It's been five hours since I kissed him goodbye and skipped like a schoolgirl through the side streets of his city.

The Chinese owner-man at the cheap Chinese restaurant I am sitting at in my sketchy neighborhood brings me my beer.

"Happy New Year," he says to me.

"Happy New Year," I manage to mutter. I am pissed-as-hell at Omar and am in no mood for pleasantries. "Thank you."

"It is on the house for you because...for New Year!" he announces, with a big smile. I know he was about to say, "Because you are alone, sad and pathetic," but he stopped himself.

"Thank you so much," I respond, desperately holding in the tears. This little kindness almost makes me cry. Little kindnesses when I'm vulnerable always do. But it's okay, because I have been sitting here already crying for ten minutes and he knows it. What's a few more tears among relative strangers?

The owner walks away and my phone *rings* this time. What do you know? It's not a text. Omar is actually *calling* me, always a rarity with my refugee. I still don't pick up. It's not this easy, Omar. You don't get off this easy. I am not *ready* to talk to you yet.

Omar kept me waiting in the cold train station for almost an hour tonight—on *New Year's Eve.* New Year's Eve! Apparently he was stuck Skyping with his fiancé for a long time. Fiancé. Shit. He *still* has a fiancé. Nothing has changed. I take a swig of my beer.

After we split late this afternoon on the train, we were to meet at 7 p.m. in the train station and head into downtown Vancouver. He texted 'make it 8 p.m.' I was annoyed, but fine: 8 p.m. it is. Then I was at the assigned meeting place—the underground, cold train, with the laughing partygoers and drunk homeless—until 9 p.m. No message, no call, no Omar. Blown. Off. I kept coming in and out of the station entrance, repaying the fare just so I could make sure I was getting a cell signal. Nada. Oh, and it was freezing. Did I mention that? I was freezing and with each passing moment, getting more and more angry. *And* I was wearing heels. Heels!

I take another drink.

He can't call? He can't text? He can't keep time? He can't hang up on his stupid *fake* fiancé and say, "I have to go meet my *real* American love?" I can't believe I am even uttering that statement. He has a fiancé, Kim!! Arranged or not! And he's blowing you off for her. Can you blame him? He *should* blow you off! She's his *fiancé*! This visit changed nothing.

I swig again, downing almost the rest of my pity beer. Beer is good. I like beer. I should drink more beer. After all, here I am in Vancouver, alone, on New Year's Eve. I start to think: if anyone else did this to me I would be mad, but not *this* mad. I'm really super insanely mad. What's going on right now? Why am I losing-my-mind-mad?

Here's the thing: I think I am three-years-mad. I think I am three-years-of-disappointment-frustration-and-heartache-mad. This isn't just about tonight. Oh my Lord!! Suddenly it all surges and I am mad-as-hell. This is about all of it—the missed yahoo appointments, the missed phone calls, the disappearing acts, the break-up text, the K1 phone call, the Bolt Bus news, the not-choosing-me, the never-prioritizing-me. This is about always feeling secondary to everything going on—his survival, his mother, a revolution. I know that sounds ridiculous, but it's the truth. Finally. He *never* loved me enough to overcome all we needed to overcome.

Wooh. There's something. Who just said that? He never loved me enough to fight for me.

I sit there a moment with that thought.

My food arrives and I look at it. Noodles. Still extremely hungry, despite the huge emotional revelation, I slowly begin to eat. Damn. It is amazing. So with Canadian-Chinese food in my mouth, I eat with the new knowledge that even here in Vancouver, Omar *still* doesn't love me enough.

I slurp more noodles and finish my beer.

Omar texts again. I ignore again. Not yet, Omar. You have to wait. I finish my food, wipe my tears and decide to go into downtown by myself. I will salvage this evening. I will. I don't need him.

"Do not bother feeding us, mother. We are dead already."

It's forty-five minutes before the New Year in the middle of about twelve thousand people in downtown Vancouver.

"I feel like I am stuck between you and Shadiya!" Omar shouted at me.

"Because you are!" I said.

He turned and walked away from me.

Following him, I shout back, "You *are* between us, Omar. What did you think? This is our situation! We both walked into this eyes open."

"My God, this is like a movie." He takes my hand and starts to walk us out of the mass of people now staring at the crazy-yelling-people on New Year's Eve. I'm not ready to hold his hand yet and I yank it back.

"Please, Kim," he says as he tries to take my hand again.

"I can't touch you, Omar." He acquiesces and I simply walk by his side lost in my angry, you-should-have-seen-this-coming-kim thoughts. I think about how I made him wait ninety minutes tonight before I called him. It was childish, yes, but felt necessary for my sanity or pride— I'm not sure which. But it didn't seem to help as here we are, in the thick of New Year's hubbub, creating a public display of anger. I came to Vancouver for an answer and for a chance at love. That chance is slipping away before my eyes. I am so mad at him; I can't see straight. We walk a block in silence.

"Where are we going?" I petulantly ask.

"I need food. I am hungry," he responds. This sets me off again.

"Well, you wouldn't be hungry if you didn't keep me waiting for hours, standing me up for our dinner date, because you would have *had* dinner with me!"

"Kim." Omar stops walking and looks at me, exhaling. "I told you. Shadiya kept me online talking for almost four hours. Something going on. I not know what. She wants talk and talk. There was nothing for me to do. What should I do, Kim?"

"You should have texted me! Told me!" I almost yell again. Drunken revelers look at us with piqued curiosity. They're looking for a fight. I am not. I start to walk again. I'm getting cold again. Omar follows behind me.

"I thought you were fine. I thought you were in that bar, Kim. I did not understand you were in train. I am sorry, Kim. Please." His defense was plausible, understandable, but I'm not ready to stop being mad at him for all of this, for everything.

"Why *you* don't call *me* to tell me that you wait?" he asks.

"Because I knew you were talking to *her* and didn't want to get you in trouble, Omar. Because I couldn't believe you weren't calling me! Because I don't want to hurt you or her!" Neither of us speaks after that for a while. We just walk. We walk and walk. I think he muttered a "shukran" in there somewhere. I don't care anymore.

We're both so tired from all the emotion and drama. I wish I had worn my comfy winter boots. My feet are killing me and freezing. Omar is not worth heels, I decide.

Several blocks later he is buying an overpriced hotdog from a street vendor and says, "Kim, I'm sorry. I didn't know what to do." I pause, as I watch him put ketchup and mustard on the dog.

I wanted to say: "You should have hung up the call! You should have chosen me! Why didn't you choose me? I'm better for you than she is. We're great together! Look at us! We could do this. This could work! But it can't just be me. *You* have to *choose* me. For once, Omar, you have to choose me!"

But I didn't say any of that, couldn't say any of that. I just stood there watching him as he slowly and deliberately searched for more condiments. I wonder if this is his first American (well, okay…Canadian) hotdog. But I am too tired to ask, or care. He made his choice and it's still not me. I watch him eat his hotdog, one of my long awaited firsts.

It's disappointing, like everything.

"They can't imagine their future and I can't imagine their past."

We end up at some bar close to midnight, luckily snagging the last table. I proceed to order us several drinks and the night proceeds to get better. I cozy up against him, forgiving him, salvaging something I sense is quickly slipping away, like Cinderella approaching the end of her night. At midnight, amidst the noisemakers and party hats, he kisses me. "Happy New Year, Kim."

"Happy New Year, Omar," I respond. It's a new beginning—and the end. I think we both feel it. And then ironically his phone rings. What is she doing up already (or still) at 7 a.m. her time? She already wished him about twelve "Happy New Years" last night! She's either A. obsessive...or B. really intuitive. I'm voting C. Both. Perhaps on some level she knows her territory is being threatened, that there's a predator close by. Women are smart like that. He steps outside to take the call. I've become a predator. I don't want to be a predator. This has to end. I order another drink.

Omar comes back a few minutes later and apologizes. I shrug and surrender. He is no longer mine, not that he ever was.

"Where we can dance?" he surprises me by asking the waitress as she brings our bill.

So we end the night dancing, ironically in a Middle Eastern restaurant and club at 4 a.m. We are hot, exhausted nd oddly content. We are having a melancholy-kind-of-fun, not riproaring, but lingering—as though trying to delay the inevitable. As the Middle Eastern-looking waitress brings another round, Omar, perhaps homesick, perhaps drunk, but working under a false assumption, tries fruitlessly to talk in Arabic to her.

"Um. I was born *here*," she replies, with a confused and somewhat annoyed look on her face and a glance to me for help. "I'm Canadian." Fail. We're not in Syria anymore, Toto. Omar and I laugh and stumble our way home, holding hands, clinging to the memory of something.

That night we lay in my bed together, barely touching.

"I have no memory, only sadness."

The next day, with all of Vancouver closed for the holiday, we wander through the barren, frozen streets, barely talking. We are as far from Syria as we could possibly be, in temperature and spirit. We're both so deep in our thoughts and so far from each other. I notice he no longer holds my hand to cross the streets. We run individually across the intersection now, instead of as one. That makes me indescribably sad. We continue to walk in this frozen tundra down to the river, silent and shivering.

"Look at the boats," Omar offers, finally talking, as we approach the icy shoreline. I am so freaking cold, I no longer care—about boats, about Omar, about anything. We stand in the face of the whipping wind, looking at the snowy water, silent. As Omar steps away to go look at something else, an icy tear freezes on my cheek. It's over. I finally found the end.

"I don't tell my kids stories anymore because they are all sad. Why tell sad stories?"

"I love you, Kim," Omar says to me in my ugly apartment building lobby, late that night. Then he kisses me. His lips feel soft upon mine and filled with finality. We are both crying again. It is early. Just ten minutes ago, we were sitting up in my rented room on my rented bed and I told my rented lover that I thought he should go back to his own apartment tonight. He did not disagree. He put on his boots and coat and hat—his *winter* clothes—and here we are, standing in the lobby saying goodbye, the same lobby where we met three short days earlier. Apparently everything between us comes in threes.

My face is in his hands. I look up at his eyes, those deep, dark, Iraqi eyes one last time. "I love you too, Omar," I say. And then he lets go of my face, turns and leaves. He simply walks out—three years, two visas and one fiancé later. He simply starts for home, his new home. And I collapse on the bench, smoke in my eyes and in my heart, sobbing in this stupid, ugly lobby—alone.

It's finally over.

Epilogue - Three Months Later

So here we are at the end of my story. But if this isn't a love story, what is it? A story of redemption? His or mine?

Maybe I was the one who needed saving. Omar didn't need saving. He got to safety on his own. He didn't need the artist visa. He didn't need the fiancé visa. He didn't even need me in the end. He never chose me. But I persisted. I persisted long after most other women would have walked away. I believed when he didn't. I believed enough for both of us, for everyone. I believed—perhaps more than I should have.

I should have known the day I left Syria that it was over. Or that it should have been. You saw that. I just refused to believe it. I refused to believe for three years. I fought like hell for the miraculous, cross-cultural storybook romance. Like a good fairytale, I wanted desperately to believe it could and would happen. Love conquers all! But it doesn't and it didn't. Sometimes love can't overcome culture or custom, family or fiancé. Sometimes love isn't enough.

And now, looking back through a lens of total transparency with the clarity of time and distance, I think I feared on some level that if I gave up Omar, my one Iraqi, it would mean eventually having to give up all the Iraqis. And I wasn't willing to do that. I wasn't willing to give up on Iraq. Omar was my link to that world, to the people.

I couldn't and still can't let go of Fakher and Saleema, of Ali, of Sawssan and Mohammed, of Shukraan, Sarah, Hatm and all of the Iraqis who shared their stories and lives with me over tea; cup after cup of damn tea. Someone needs to remember these people who shared their pain and devastation, fears and tears. Someone needs to remember the stories. Hanging onto Omar was perhaps a way to hang on to them, because as he so brutally reminded me, Omar was one of "those Iraqis"—a refugee. Omar is a refugee.

He just also happens to be the one refugee I loved. Yes, I did love Omar. And he loved me.

And as for the rest of the Iraqis I met? It is to them I am most grateful—for their generosity, for their hopefulness, for their faith in humanity and mostly for their faith in me.

At least I get an ending. That's more than the millions of Iraqis who are still waiting—languishing, destitute and running out of hope—can say. Where is their ending? It seems there is no end to the pain and suffering of innocent people—even today, years later. Somalia. South Sudan and of course Syria. Poor Syria. There is no end to the Diaspora of a people and their culture. There is no end to the killings and kidnappings and to the sad, sad stories. There are more than sixty-five million refugees worldwide and we continue to turn our backs and hearts, forgetting it could be any one of us at any time; that we are them, that our stories are the same.

Omar was one of the lucky ones—lucky to survive the war and displacement and revolution, lucky to get a chance to start over, to begin again, lucky to love and be loved. He's one of the lucky ones. So am I. And I guess that has to be enough—for now.

So there it is.

I did as Fakher asked: I told the whole story, as I heard it and as I lived it. And now by sharing the stories with you, dear reader, sweetly, the weight on me has lightened.

Shukran, my friend. We are now family.

As we always were.

End.

Acknowledgements

This book has been nothing short of an epic journey. I want to thank so many people, without whose help along the way, writing it would not have been possible.

First and foremost, I need to thank Omar. This is his story, as much as mine. Thank you for allowing me to tell our story. Thank you for trusting me. You will always hold a piece of my heart, habibi.

I have had many editors along the way who have helped shape the book and I am grateful to them all: Laura Matthews for starting things off, Benee Knauer for the heavy lifting, Heather Edwards for believing in this story and jumping in and supporting me at a critical time, and to Randy O'Neill for the continued support and additional editorial assistance. Thank you.

Thank you also to Deborah Oster Pannell for always partnering with me on my creative projects, for being an additional editor and sounding board on this book and continually assisting in my fight to share these stories on behalf of Iraqi refugees. I am grateful you could write the introduction and for your continued presence in my artistic life.

And then, of course, huge thanks to my publisher Camilla Reeve at Palewell Press. You made me do things structurally I knew needed to be done, but struggled against for years. Thank you for finding me, pushing me in the edits and for saying yes to this story. I am happy to be published by Palewell Press and grateful the universe provided you!

None of this would have happened had the New York NGO, *Intersections International* not invited me on a little trip to the Middle East and commissioned me to write a play. Thank you to Rev. Robert Chase, C. Eduardo Vargas and Megan Hoelle for trusting me with these powerful stories and initiating the change in me created these past seven years. I am different because of you.

Thanks also to the collaborators on my play, *No Place Called Home*, which eventually became inspiration for this book: Sarah Cameron Sunde for your brave and crucial direction and partnership on the play, as well as musician and person extraordinaire, Amikaeyla Gaston. What we did together made me realize I needed to share the wider story in book form. I am deeply grateful to you both. Thanks also to all the seven other artist collaborators with whom I shared Jordan, Lebanon and Syria, as well as the weight of the stories we were told.

Acknowledgements

I am grateful to the aid organizations we met with doing the heavy footwork in the countries we visited: UNHCR, Caritas International, Mercy Corps, RESTART and the Center for Victims of Torture. Thank you for the continued work you do, as well as allowing us to peer into the lives devastated by war.

Thanks also to organizations I mention, in this book, having worked with including *The List Project* and *Iraqi Student Project*—two amazing organizations that did amazing work at a crucial time.

Many thanks to Monica Haller and *The Veterans Book Project* for asking me to write the small documentation, *Story Diary*, recounting my experience in the Middle East in journal form. That book led to this one. Thank you for allowing me to share my story and for the work you do on behalf of Veterans and Iraqis.

Oddly, this book was started and finished in Mexico and I am grateful to the country for its hospitality, as well as to Erin Ko and Alec Von Bargen for hosting me as I began the book and to Monica King and Jennifer Smith for providing a space to finish it.

Gratitude also to my mom for being along on this wild ride and supporting me the whole way.

But mostly, thank you to the Iraqis, the hundreds of Iraqis who shared their stories with me over tea. It is you to whom I am most grateful and most indebted and to whom I hope I honored in the telling of your stories. Shukran, my friends.

We owe so much more to the 65 million refugees worldwide than we are providing. May this book be a step forward in recognizing their humanity and our own.

Kim Schultz is a Chicago based author, actor and refugee advocate. In 2009, she travelled to the Middle East as an artist/activist to meet with Iraqi refugees, falling in love with Omar and forever changing her life. For the past seven years, inspired to work on behalf of refugees worldwide, Kim began promoting the art of displaced Iraqi artists, working as NY Chapter Chair of *The List Project* as well as helping recently resettled refugees make a home in the U.S. through various resettlement organizations. Artistically, she turned their stories and her own into a critically-acclaimed play *No Place Called Home: This Isn't Supposed to be a Love Story*, a small journal style book *Story Diary* (Veterans Book Project, 2012) and the memoir *Three Days in Damascus* (Palewell Press, 2016). Kim has published several articles and op-eds on the subject and has an essay published in *Chicken Soup for the Soul: Angels and Miracles* (Chicken Soup for the Soul, 2016). She blogs, tweets and can be generally found at kimschultz.net and www.3daysindamascus.com

For more information on the play *No Place Called Home*, please visit www.omarwashisname.blogspot.com

Story Diary, Kim Schultz's first book on the subject of Iraqi refugees can be found at www.veteransbookproject.com

Organizations the author has worked with:

www.intersectionsinternational.org

www.thelistproject.org

www.iraqistudentproject.org

www.veteransbookproject.com

Moved to do more?

In addition to the good organizations mentioned in the acknowledgements, here are some additional smaller organizations working hard on behalf of refugees worldwide:

www.epic-usa.org

www.reconciliationproject.org

www.karamfoundation.org

www.girlforward.org

www.collateralrepairproject.org

Palewell Press

Palewell Press is a small independent publisher handling poetry, fiction and non-fiction with a particular interest in human rights, social history, and the environment. You can reach the editor via enquiries@palewellpress.co.uk

Lightning Source UK Ltd.
Milton Keynes UK
UKOW05f1807041216
289178UK00003BA/99/P